The Philosophy of Right and Wrong

The Philosophy of Right and Wrong

An Introduction to Ethical Theory

BERNARD MAYO

ROUTLEDGE & KEGAN PAUL

London and New York

First published in 1986
by Routledge & Kegan Paul plc

11 New Fetter Lane, London EC4P 4EE

Published in the USA by
Routledge & Kegan Paul Inc.
in association with Methuen Inc.
29 West 35th Street, New York, NY 10001

Set in 10 on 12 pt Palatino
by Inforum Ltd, Portsmouth
and printed in Great Britain
by T J Press (Padstow) Ltd
Padstow, Cornwall

Library of Congress Cataloging in Publication Data

Mayo, Bernard.
    The philosophy of right and wrong.
    Bibliography: p.
    Includes index.
    1. Ethics.   I. Title.
BJ1012.M39   1986   171'.2   85–28108

ISBN 0–7102–0851–0 (c)
ISBN 0–7102–0859–6 (p)

British Library CIP Data also available

Contents

My thanks are due especially to Ted Honderich, without whose firm encouragement this book would not have appeared.

CHAPTER I

Introduction

Is ethics, or moral philosophy, a practical or a theoretical subject? It will be obvious from the outset that this volume is not a practical handbook. It does not contain instructions on how to be good. But there must be a question about this. What is the difference, and the relation, between practical and theoretical ethics? For of course there is such a thing as practical ethics: there is such a thing as learning how to be good, how to act rightly, and so on; only it doesn't happen to be a subject that is taught in academic institutions or in their textbooks. Nor is it taught anywhere else, apparently; and we might well start by asking why not. This in fact is the very question that Plato asked in his dialogue, the *Meno*. His problem was, that there were plenty of teachers available in subjects like mathematics and medicine, but there was a puzzling shortage, indeed a total absence, of teachers in the subject of goodness or virtue. And this was paradoxical, for the following reason. While of course it's important that someone who wants to become a doctor should learn to be a good doctor, surely it is much *more* important that he, and everyone else, should learn to be a good *man* (or, we might add today, woman[1]). What makes the paradox even sharper is that this is the one practical question that is literally inescapable. For we can escape every other practical question: we can escape the practical question of how to become a good doctor, by simply choosing another profession. But since we cannot choose not to be human beings, we cannot escape the question of how to be good, rather than bad, ones.

We can see at once that the question, why are there no courses in practical ethics (either here and now, or in Plato's society) is not itself a practical question. That is, we don't expect the answer to be anything like the sort of answer that would apply to questions about why there are no courses in Italian at some institutions, or no teachers of Chemical Engineering. The answer cannot be anything remotely like: because the Government is too mean to allocate money for the foundation of a Chair of Goodness, or a Department of Right Conduct, in some university. Rather, the answer will have to be to the effect that goodness, or right conduct, is not the sort of thing that can be taught by means of books or lectures. This immediately raises three questions:

(1) How then *is* morality taught? After all, we *do* 'learn' to be good.
(2) What *is* there about the nature of goodness and rightness which makes it impossible to teach in formal institutions?
(3) What *is* taught, or studied, in institutions of learning under the title of ethics?

To answer question 1, we must note that when I said that morality is taught, or learnt, there is something odd about this teaching and learning – hence my quotation-marks above. All that it is really safe to say is that morality is *acquired* and *imparted*; that we do become more or less decent men and women as a result of *some* early processing: by some form of interaction between ourselves and others who already have their moral standards and practices. These people we may call moralists. They may be parents, preachers, or teachers – and by teachers I mean those who teach *other* things. The mathematics teacher teaches mathematics, but he may set a moral example too, for instance in truthfulness and integrity. We can sum up this process of imparting goodness, by contrast with teaching it, as the method of *precept* and *example*.

Next, question 3. What *is* propounded in books or courses like this one is ethical *theory*, or *theoretical* ethics, or moral philosophy. And one of the main lines of enquiry of this philosophical

[2]

discipline just is Plato's question, that is, question 2, and related questions about the nature of morality.

What we are chiefly concerned with, then, are questions about the nature of morality. Often these questions will take the form of investigating moral language and moral concepts; and when they do, it will be clear that we are then engaged in a theoretical study, because studying language is quite different from using it. Now one might feel uncomfortable about this. It is not committing us to too sharp a distinction between theory and practice? Surely there must be some practical relevance, some non-theoretical value, in the theory? This is a question on which opinions have long been sharply divided. To give some idea of the opposing views, we can start again with Plato. We have seen him raising the theoretical questions in the *Meno*: but in the *Republic*, the major work to which the *Meno* is often regarded as a preamble, Plato leaves us in no doubt about practical import: he says 'We are not engaged in a casual enquiry, but in the question, what is the right way to live'; he claims that philosophers ought to be rulers (and vice versa); and that virtue is knowledge. By contrast, we can take two British philosophers. John Stuart Mill, writing to a lady who asked his advice as a philosopher as to whether she ought to leave her husband, replied 'Philosophical qualities do not include that of being a competent adviser and director of consciences in the most difficult affairs of private life'; while G.E. Moore, in *Principia Ethica*, says 'What I am concerned with is knowledge only – that we should think correctly and arrive at some truth, however unimportant; I do not say that such knowledge will make us more useful members of society. If anyone does not care for knowledge for its own sake, then I have nothing to say to him.'

It appears that the relation between theory and practice in ethics is very much in dispute. Consider a very closely related distinction: the distinction between fact and value, between what is and what ought to be. This is a closely related distinction, because facts are what we theorise about, while values are what guide our practice. On the face of it, there is not only a difference, but a troublesome contrast, which has been a problem for philosophers since at least the time of Socrates. It is only too obvious that, generally speaking, the facts are not what they should be, and what ought to be is not in fact the case; what ought not to be, all too often is. Some philosophers, such as Hume (at least on one standard interpretation), have been content to accept, even to insist on, the absolute duality of the Is and the Ought; others have tried to cross the Is-Ought gap in some way. Since Plato, for example, philosophers have tried to think of values as some special sort of facts. If values were indeed some very special sort of facts, then the way would be open for a systematic study of values which might take its place as a science alongside the other sciences. There would be a programme for two kinds of science: the ordinary empirical sciences which deal with what can be known by observation and theory, and the normative sciences, which would deal with what can be known by attending to our experiences of valuing.

This programmatic science of value would have to be sharply distinguished from a quite different kind of normative science which does actually exist as an ordinary empirical science, but does not, unfortunately, have the right subject for the programme. This is the science *of norms*: that is, the systematic study of the rules, codes, principles, customs and practices which are actually followed in particular societies, as studied, for instance, by social anthropologists. Now these norms are indeed a certain kind of fact, and can indeed be studied; but what makes them the wrong subject for the supposed science of values is that they are only the facts of what people *think* ought to be done, not facts of what *ought* to be done: what people actually value, as opposed to what they ought to value.

Needless to say, the programme of developing a science of value which would disclose the facts of what really ought to be done, what principles we really ought to live by, has made remarkably little progress, and it is not surprising that many philosophers have decided that there can be no such science because the whole idea is radically misconceived. To speak of a 'systematic search for the principles of wise choice' sounds very appealing, but, according to the critics, this is just an illicit combination of two incompatible things, a theoretical system or science, and a set of principles to live by, which cannot be a science.

[4]

Yet we can hardly leave the matter there. The fact is that the 'theoretical isolationist' view has come under increasing attack in recent times. Modern writers on ethics, such as John Rawls, Bernard Williams, and Mary Midgley, certainly claim to be doing ethics of a kind highly relevant to practical life. Journals and institutions devoted to such notions as 'Philosophy and Public Affairs' abound. My quotation from John Stuart Mill (p.3), it will be said, was perversely beside the point: Mill's refusal to advise on a particular, personal problem is entirely outweighed by the enormous, and quite intentional, influence of his political philosophy on the public affairs of Victorian Britain. There was indeed a truly isolationist period typified by Moore, Ayer and Stevenson, but this, it is urged, was an aberration from which we have now escaped (and to which, it may be added, the Continental philosophers never succumbed).

What is the case for theoretical isolationism? I think there is only one argument, which is powerful but not conclusive. It rests on the very nature of philosophy itself. There must be something *distinctive* about a philosophical treatment of morality, as opposed, say, to that of a scientist, a preacher, or the common man. And what is distinctive about philosophy is that it is a *second-order* discipline. To see the force of this, I shall give the strongest version of what it has been held to mean.

Philosophy as a meta-subject

In attempting to characterise what is distinctive of philosophy, the first thing to emphasise is *enquiry*. The very word has this element built-in from the start; it was invented by Pythagoras, and there are two implications. First, there is the idea of *disinterested curiosity* (compare the quotation from Moore about knowledge for its own sake). Second, the idea of pursuit as opposed to possession. Philosophy is not wisdom, not a body of knowledge. Of course the idea of pursuing wisdom or knowledge suggests the idea of a goal which a successful pursuit would attain. But the only thing that all philosophers have in common is an unusually determined attempt to think out solutions to unusually recalcitrant problems. But what kind of problems? The answer I shall give to this question is the one that leads to isolationism.

Philosophy is the discussion of theoretical problems which cannot have theoretical answers; that is to say, they cannot have answers in terms of the theory in which they arise, but only in terms of another theory, namely philosophy. Some well-known examples will illustrate this point. (1) This table is solid, dense, stable, thoroughly visible and tangible; yet according to the physicists it consists almost entirely of empty space with small particles moving rapidly and entirely inaccessible to the senses. Which is the real table? (2) (A celebrated problem of Bertrand Russell.) We all know that certain things happened in the past, we have our memories and our history books. But couldn't our memories be entirely deceptive, and couldn't all the historical evidence be fraudulent? How can I be sure that I didn't spring into existence five minutes ago, complete with memories of a wholly unreal past? (Notice that just this kind of thesis was actually held by those Fundamentalists who claimed that God created, in 4004 BC, among other things, fossils which were not caused by growth in earlier seasons.) (3) Suppose that I am an only child. Suppose that my parents in fact had never met, but each of them had met and married someone else, and each couple had just one child. Which child would have been me? (4) The problem of free will (to be dealt with at length later).

What all these problems have in common is that each of them arises out of a certain theoretical field of enquiry: (1) arises from physics; (2) from history and geology; (3) from genetics and psychology; (4) from physics and physiology. Moreover, what actually makes them problems is very often a conflict between theory and common sense, as with (1) and (4).

So philosophy, on this view, is a receptacle for an unlimited number of miscellaneous problems thrown up by other disciplines. This explains why it has no specific subject-matter of its own: because anything and everything is its subject-matter, though only after it has been already processed by theoretical thinking. For philosophy is not thinking about raw data, but thinking about the products of thinking itself. For this reason it is sometimes called a 'meta-subject'. The word 'meta' means in Greek simply 'after', and it occurs first, in philosophy, as the title of Aristotle's work *The Metaphysics*. This work was not named by Aristotle himself, but by a later editor, who simply published it *after The Physics*, as 'Physics Volume II', as it were. But since it does contain more philosophy than the *Physics* does, this was a happy accident: it perpetuates the idea that philosophical problems come *after* physical or mathematical or historical ones, because they arise out of them. So they are sometimes called meta-mathematical or meta-historical problems. And *if* there are problems arising out of moral thinking, which are the subject of moral philosophy or ethics, they will be meta-moral problems. But, just as the philosopher of history is not doing history, so, it appears, the moral philosophers will not be engaged in moralising.

Before I turn to these meta-moral problems, something must be said about a third distinctive feature of philosophy: its method. The method is simply, rational discussion. Of course this is not a distinctive feature, since rational discussion is common to all the academic disciplines. What makes it a distinctive feature is to add 'rational discussion *and only* rational discussion': for it *is* distinctive of philosophy, on this view, that it does not involve any observations or (if there are non-observational facts, as in mathematics) factual investigations. A more positive way of putting this negative point is to use the phrase 'conceptual analysis': if philosophy is thinking about (the products of) thinking, it will be examining, criticising, analysing *concepts* rather than things. This point can be illustrated by the elementary schoolboy puzzle (which could be added to the list of problems above, though it is too elementary to count as philosophical) about what happens when an irresistible cannon-ball meets an immovable post. It is perfectly clear that the answer is not a factual investigation but a conceptual analysis.

Returning now to the question of meta-problems: are there meta-moral problems? In all the four examples, the theory out of which a problem arose was indeed a theory, a science. And all the sciences are concerned with truth. But there are other fields of activity which are not concerned with truth, but with things equally important in human life. We are concerned to do what is right, to fulfil our obligations, to be morally good men and women. Again we may wish to write, or to appreciate, music, or poetry, or to be creative, or critical, in other fields of art. So there are activities concerned with what is good or beautiful, and it is not surprising that in traditional philosophy the Good and the Beautiful have figured alongside Truth as ultimate objects of pursuit. (Here another link was found between fact and value: not only were values a special sort of facts, but Truth, which all factual enquiries pursue, is itself a value.)

Now meta-problems, as we have seen, arise out of various fields of *thinking*; but morality (and art) is a field of practical *activity*. There are, obviously enough, practical moral problems; but how can there be theoretical problems, as material for the moral philosopher? The answer is that morality cannot be *merely* a field of practical activity. Morality necessarily involves moral thinking as well as moral action; and the meta-problems, the philosophy, develop from the thinking, not the acting. There is no such thing, at least as far as the moral philosopher is concerned, as a moral action which is just an action. (As a matter of fact there is not really a contrast with science here, despite the difference between theory and practice. For theory itself requires activity: not merely intellectual activity, but manual, such as experiments and diggings. But experimenting is not just tinkering with apparatus, and archaeology is not just making holes in the ground; both activities control, and are controlled by, some theoretical purpose.) So morality is not just a way of behaving, but a way of thinking about behaving. Sometimes, indeed, we may just act without thinking. But sometimes we think about what we are doing, or have done, or will do, where there is no question of our own activity. And sometimes this thinking is moral thinking. (It is often assumed that it is moral thinking when we use words like 'ought', 'right' or 'good', but this is a mistake, for we use these words in non-moral thinking too.)

We can sum up in terms of three levels: acting, thinking, and philosophising. The person who simply acts we may call the Agent. The only question at his level is 'What shall I do?', and since he is not doing any further thinking, he answers this question by going ahead and doing X whatever it may be. He cannot be called a *moral* agent at this stage.

The person who thinks about what someone is doing we may call the Spectator, or Commentator; and if he thinks critically he will be a critic or judge; if he thinks in terms of moral concepts he will be a moral critic or Moralist. His question is not 'What shall I do?', but 'What should he do, or have done?'; and, since he can of course be a critic of his own actions, 'What *should* I do, or have done?'; and if the question is what he or I *morally* should do, then he is a moral critic. Moral problems (as opposed to questions) arise only at this second level. One large class of examples of moral problem-situations is that known as Conflict of Duties. Plato gives a good example in the opening pages of the *Republic*: ought I to return a borrowed weapon if I have good reason to think its owner will do harm with it? This is a conflict between the duty to keep promises and the duty to prevent avoidable harm. Another familiar example is the conflict between the demands of justice and of mercy, as in *The Merchant of Venice*.

The moral philosopher is thinking (third level) about thinking (second level), and this is thinking of a different *order*. Both first and second levels represent our common moral consciousness, and its problems are those of *first-order* ethics; philosophy, by contrast, is a *second-order* discipline, or a meta-subject, because it is concerned with the concepts which typically occur in the (first-order) thinking of the moral agents and critics.

Here are three second-order questions which a modern philosopher sees as the three fundamental questions for moral philosophy:[2]

(1) Why do we do what is right?

(2) Why should we do what is right?

(3) How do we know what is right?

And I wish to add a fourth:

(4) What do we mean by 'right'?

As a small example of the 'conceptual analysis' approach, consider how we might deal with someone who claimed to have an instant set of answers to all four questions. He might point out that a perfectly ordinary word, in common use, gives us a complete solution. The word occurred in the Mill quotation: it is the word 'Conscience'. We *do* what is right because our conscience tells us to, and we usually obey our conscience, because if we don't we suffer remorse. We *should* do what is right, because it is of the nature of conscience to be a proper authority. We *know* what is right by consulting our conscience, which is either infallible or at least usually correct, indeed perhaps the voice of God. And 'right' simply *means* what our conscience prescribes, 'wrong' what it forbids. Now these answers, we must surely suspect, are far too true to be good. It is all too common a fault to invent a purely verbal explanation, by naming an entity which, if it existed, would solve a problem, but there is no independent reason for thinking that it does exist. This is not just a philosophical error; there have been examples in the history of science, such as the dormitive property of opium, the luminiferous ether, phlogiston, and centrifugal force.

This concludes the case for theoretical isolationism based on (a certain view of) the nature of philosophy as a distinctive, second-order discipline. On this view, it may be conceded that the clear and rigorous thinking required in this discipline will be beneficial for any philosopher who happens to be also interested in the first-order problems of morality, but that there is no closer connection between theory and practice. And I must confess that I do not know of any radically different, but acceptable, view of the distinctive nature of philosophy from which any closer connection *would* follow. It will not do, for instance, to fall back on the lame truism that philosophy is 'an unusually determined effort to think clearly'[3] – this reduces a difference of kind to one of mere degree. Nevertheless it may turn out that the combination of second-order thinking, analytical rigour, practical first-order expertise and a deep concern for first-order issues, may itself constitute a distinctive nature.

I shall therefore make a fresh start by leaving aside these methodological matters, and address a particular specimen problem in the hope that the course of our discussion will bring out more clearly the kind of thing we are doing. It is one of the few genuinely philosophical problems that many people unversed in philosophy have actually thought about (another is the free will problem). But people who have thought about it have all too often either got the wrong answer, or they have got the right answer but for the wrong reason. This is the problem of *objectiv-*

ity: whether moral judgments are objective or subjective; that is, whether they are true (or false) independently of who happens to be making them. Is there a real basis for moral judgment, or is it all a matter of personal feelings or attitudes? (These may not be the only alternatives.) Here is how the problem surfaces even in a work of light fiction:

'Do you know what you've gone and done, Cary? You've developed a personal sense of justice. You think that what you think is right, *is* right.'

'I have to, Judd. I haven't got anyone else to tell me.'[4]

Too many people are apt to say, having thought about the question a little, things like 'Ethics is a matter of opinion', 'Morality is intensely personal', 'Moral judgments can only be subjective'. They take the position that Judd reproaches Cary for having. ('Morality is intensely personal' was actually said to me by a first-year philosophy student who was known to devote herself to worthy causes outside the lecture room, and seemed quite unconscious of the contradiction.) Yet each of these remarks can have a certain truth, but it does *not* follow that subjectivism in ethics is a true thesis. These people have got hold of the right sort of reasons – it is true, as Cary says, that you can't be *told* what is right by someone else – but their conclusion is wrong. On the other hand, too many people are also apt to say that of course morality is not subjective. They take Judd's position. These people have got the right answer, but usually for the wrong reasons. The reasons are that they have not been thinking deeply at all, but are just reacting to the way they have been brought up. And *of course* we are not brought up to think that the moral teaching we receive from our parents and other mentors is *merely* the personal opinions of those particular individuals, any more than we are expected to take our history lessons as merely the personal opinions of our history teachers.

There is another reason why I mention this problem in this introductory chapter. A recent influential textbook by John Mackie, *Ethics*, appears – and the appearance is confirmed by the provocative sub-title, *Inventing Right and Wrong* – to be advocating what I have just described as the wrong answer, ethical subjectivism. Now even if he were advocating the wrong answer, this would not necessarily detract from his value as a textbook. What is important in philosophy is to follow arguments critically, and a very good way of practising this to take an argument leading to a conclusion you are not prepared to accept. You are much more likely to find something wrong with the argument. So we needn't worry if Mackie's conclusion is unacceptable. Hardly anyone accepts any of Plato's philosophical conclusions, yet this doesn't detract from Plato's status as the greatest philosopher. But to return to Mackie: I said that he *appears* to be advocating the wrong conclusion, but in fact he isn't, if we follow him carefully. The point is that the pair of terms 'objective' and 'subjective' admit of different shades of meaning, are very difficult to define precisely, and even philosophers use them in different ways. It turns out that the ethical subjectivism that Mackie advocates is so extremely weak that I prefer to call it something else. It certainly isn't what the unsophisticated subjectivists in the last paragraph had in mind.

It is as well to remind ourselves again that there are values and value-judgments other than moral ones. There are, for instance, aesthetic values, and the same problem arises there. One might think at first that there are stronger pressures towards subjectivism in this area, perhaps because works of art are artificial products and we are not; perhaps because we speak of *taste* in this area and the remark 'it's a matter of taste' is an explicit disclaimer of objectivity. Yet, paradoxically, there are also stronger pressures towards objectivity. Contrasting with the fact, dwelt on earlier, that there are no handbooks or taught courses in either practical ethics or moral criticism, is the fact that a whole range of academic disciplines requires standards of literary criticism and even creative activity. How can there be Arts Faculties or works of literary criticism if all judgment is subjective? But this would be a subject for another book.

To resume, then: let us look again at the problem of moral values and their objectivity, by comparing them, not with aesthetic values, but with a third set. This will also help us to see how moral philosophy is related to other major branches of philosophy. These are the branches, such as Logic, and Theory of Knowledge, and (most of) Metaphysics, which are concerned with the values Truth and Falsity; or, rather, to be more accurate and non-committal, with our concern for the true and the false. (We include negative values, that is, those we are concerned to avoid or minimise.) Moral philosophy, likewise, is concerned with our concern for right and wrong, good and evil. How basic are these concerns in human life? (The more basic they are, the more likely that there is something objective about them). How important, for instance, is truth? How important it is can be brought out by the following conversation:

'What's your favourite subject?'

'History.'

'What particularly interests you in, say, recent European history?'

'Well, the German occupation of Britain in 1940.'

'But it's not true that Germany occupied Britain in 1940.'

'I know it's not *true*, but that's not what you asked me. It's *interesting*, and that's what you did ask me, isn't it?'

Now one side of this conversation is incoherent. The speaker has shown that he cannot distinguish between history and fiction; and anyone who can't do this can't know what history (or fiction) actually is. One can't be interested in anything that admits of being true or false without being *concerned whether* it is true, or false; and this is our concern for truth. What, then, about morality? Let us construct another imaginary conversation:

'What's your favourite occupation?'

'Dealing with people.'

'What sort of dealing do you prefer?'

'Torturing.'

'But it's wrong to torture people.'

'I know it's *wrong*, but that's not what you asked me. I *like* it, and that's what you did ask me, isn't it?'

Again, one side of this conversation is incoherent. This time the speaker has shown that he can't distinguish between personal inclinations and matters of right and wrong; and anyone who can't do that can't know the meaning of right and wrong. One can't admit that something is wrong while saying in the same breath that one doesn't care whether it is or not.

Another way of comparing the two areas of philosophy, the

philosophy of theory and the philosophy of practice, is to note that philosophy often begins with scepticism. (In fact subjectivism is just one variety of scepticism.) There are many examples of scepticism among the classical philosophers in the area of truth and knowledge. Descartes, for instance, speculated on the possibility that our entire knowledge of the external world might be an illusion: either a dream, or a set of false beliefs induced in us by a malignant demon. Another, more recent, example links up with our historian. It is question (2) on p.6: how do we know that the whole world didn't come into existence five minutes ago, complete with fossils, socks with holes in them, and memories, all of them false indicators of a past which never existed? These strange possibilities force us to do some hard thinking about the foundation of our claims to know things.

So in morals. Isn't it possible that the whole system of Greco-Judaeo-Christian ethics, which is at the centre of all moral thinking in the Western world, could be entirely perverted? Couldn't it be that we really ought not to love our neighbour, but that we ought to hate him instead? Couldn't there be a 'Satanic' morality, just the reverse of ours? Or just no morals at all? Indeed both these possibilities might seem less far-fetched than the ones about knowledge. Certainly they force us to do some hard thinking about the foundations of ethics. But notice that even the sceptical possibilities, except perhaps the last, assume a certain objectivity.

But has the preceding discussion of the objectivity issue helped to answer our original question about the practical relevance of moral philosophy? So far, it appears not. Our discussion was a theoretical one. An actual moral 'issue', whether or not it is wrong to torture people, was simply assumed to be settled. Our conclusions were entirely neutral as between different views in (first-order) ethics. It *might* be held that a theoretical discussion leading to an assurance that our moral views are a matter of objectivity *might* be practically relevant, in, for example, increasing our confidence in believing, advocating and practising them. But it is not clear why it should, and in any case this possible confidence-boosting effect is far less than is claimed by the opponents of isolationism.

To see the real case against isolationism, we must revise our initial classification of two orders of questions, and introduce a third. So far we have assumed that questions concerning morals split into the following types:

A (1) Ought I to divorce my husband?
A (2) Should Mrs Smith evict her lodger?
and
B (1) Is morality reducible to self-interest?
B (2) Does 'right' mean 'whatever produces the most good'?

These are all (typically) difficult questions, and there are important differences between the difficulties in A and those in B. So far we have taken this to mean that moral philosophy is only about questions of type B, and not at all about questions of type A. This was the attractively simple distinction between primary or first-order ethics (type A) and second-order or meta-ethics (type B). Questions of type A, it was suggested, are not answered by moral philosophers but by moralists. What the philosopher is concerned with, on this view, was not the primary questions, but such things as the key concepts which figure in both the questions and the answers, and questions about these are type B questions. Even our discussion of subjectivism belongs to this level: we should enter the question 'Are moral judgments subjective or objective?' in the B-list above.

However, this attractively simple distinction, with its perhaps less attractive consequence of isolationism, will in any case not work. We have ignored (perversely, some will say) a third type of questions, which we must now introduce:

C Questions about *major general* issues, such as the rights and wrongs of: abortion, eating animals, euthanasia, obscenity, punishment of criminals, warfare.

These issues may be summed up, more or less literally, as matters of life and death. They are not practical questions like the A-type questions, though of course they have practical implications. If I believe that war is an unqualified evil, then of course this has the practical consequence that I must refuse military service. But doing this is acting at the level of a type-A question, whereas the original question, about war in general, is not. (I may, after all, be a woman, or disabled.) Now these general life-or-death questions

[15]

cannot be answered without some typically philosophical reflection on meanings. For instance, questions about abortion inevitably run into questions about what counts as being alive, or being a person (is a foetus a person?). Again, take the question whether a doctor is guilty of murder if he switches off a machine which is keeping a hopeless invalid technically alive but in a deep and irreversible coma. Now suppose that, instead of switching off the machine, he omits to supply one to such a patient, because the only available machine is one which could help to cure another patient. Is he guilty in both cases, in one case, or in neither? The decision here depends on very difficult philosophical questions about the meanings of certain key terms, such as acts of omission and acts of commission. Only by getting clear about such things can we decide if Ted Honderich is right, for example, in claiming that I am as guilty, in not paying for food parcels for starving Africans, as I would be if I were to send poisoned ones.[5]

Take another example from the field of warfare. Is it right to kill 100,000 people if the result is the shortening of a war and the saving of the lives of a million people? (The problem of Hiroshima, grossly over-simplified.) Some moralists would say that the deliberate killing of even one innocent person is an absolute evil, not to be redeemed by any trade-off against any amount of consequential good, or, more likely, by the averting of any amount of consequential evil. This kind of example raises difficult problems about comparing one sort of badness, the badness of evil actions, against another sort, the badness of resulting states of affairs. Now disputes about the relevance of consequences do not seem to be first-order moral problems; they call for philosophical enquiry; yet they clearly have practical implications.

We must therefore make room for two aspects of moral philosophy, not one, corresponding to the distinction between B-type and C-type questions. This book will be concerned chiefly with B-type questions, and so will move closer to the isolationist conception of moral philosophy than some readers may wish. However, before closing this chapter I will display a final example which links together both of the last two topics: the question of objectivity, which was a B-type question, and one of the C-type questions, namely the question of obscenity. The example is taken from a *Times* article on the Longford Report (the one preceding the more recent Williams report, that is).

Before obscenity can be controlled by law, it has to be defined, so that the police and magistrates can recognise cases of the obscene when they come across them. The current definition was given in the Jenkins Act of 1959, and was in terms of 'a tendency to deprave and corrupt'. Lord Longford's new definition was to be in terms of what 'outrages contemporary standards of decency or humanity accepted by the public at large', or, to abbreviate somewhat, 'what is offensive to most ordinary people'. Now, as the *Times* correspondent pointed out,

> 'the advantage of the "offensive" test is that it is essentially empirical in a way that the "depravity and corruption" test could never be. For depravity and corruption are value-terms, essentially involving judgments of value as well as of fact; but it is a simple matter of fact that we all find some things offensive. On the Longford test those things which feature on the offensiveness lists of most of our fellow-citizens will be obscene.

Now for the *Times* correspondent's own view of the matter. Lord Longford, he says, clearly implies that he is prepared to make do with such a view:

> As a devout Catholic living in a secular society this must be a matter of regret to him. The question is, *can* we make do with such a view? Do we *really* believe that our perceptions of the good and the beautiful . . . are only of relative significance? If our answer is in the affirmative, we would do well to reconsider from their foundations the purposes we deem ourselves to be fulfilling in the universities, and in relation to the higher culture which we inherit and seek to extend.

Leaving the word 'relative' for treatment elsewhere, I wish to note here that this powerful anti-subjectivist statement, while an important and true answer to a B-type question, is not an answer to the C-type question from which it arose. It does not tell us, even by implication, what we should do about obscenity.

CHAPTER II

Determinism

In the next two chapters, I want to discuss two major philosophical theories which in different ways constitute serious threats to the existence and objectivity of values. If either of them is correct, there will be little or nothing left for moral philosophy to be about; so it is important to establish that they are not correct, before going on. One of these, Determinism, is a metaphysical, not an ethical, theory, but if it is true there cannot *be* an ethical theory. The other, Emotivism, is a theory in moral philosophy, but it makes such very short work of the subject that all moral philosophy can be covered in a couple of pages. The different destructive effects of these two theories can be neatly shown by distinguishing between the *meaning* and the *application* of a word. Most words have both; they have a meaning, and there are circumstances in which they are correctly applied. But some lack one or other of these. The word 'dragon' has a perfectly good meaning, but there are no actual circumstances in which it correctly applies to anything. On the other hand, the word 'hello' is correctly applied in the circumstances of meeting someone, but it has no meaning. Now according to determinism, moral words have meaning, but no proper application; they express genuine concepts, but they suffer from the same defects as dragons, fairies or hobbits; and a treatise on fictitious concepts will have little appeal. By contrast, according to emotivism, moral words have occasions for proper application, but no meaning, and do not express genuine concepts. Words like 'hello', 'boo' and 'hurrah' are correctly applied in appropriate circumstances, there are real situations which call for their use; but of course they have no meaning. And, again, a treatise on greetings, interjections and expletives is of rather limited appeal.

First, then, the threat of determinism. Suppose we were to answer question (1) on p.9 ('Why do we do what is right?') by any of the following:

'Because we are reacting to childhood influences and conditioning';
'Because we are under social pressures to conform'; or even
'Because our movements are caused by muscular contrac-
tions which . . . '

None of these explanations seems to leave room for any 'should' or 'ought'. In fact they positively rule out the possibility of any oughts or ought-nots, because of a famous principle, due to Kant, that 'ought' implies 'can'. It only makes sense to say that I ought to do something, if it is possible for me to choose whether to do it or not to do it. I must be able to choose between alternatives; each of them must be something that I can do, and that I can refrain from doing. But if everything I do is an effect of causes outside my control, then there never are such alternatives: whenever I do anything, the only thing I 'can' do is the one thing I *do* do, and that means that I can't choose whether to do it or not.

Let us look again at question (1). I have just shown that it could be answered as if it were a question about causes, in terms of the determinants of norm-conformity. But it could also be taken as a question about *reasons*; and to take it that way is to ask about our thinking; it is to ask, in effect, question (2): 'Why *should* we do what is right', taken as 'Why do we think we should do what we think is right?'. Now if this is a genuine question, there must be some real connection between what we think and what we do: between knowing or believing that something is right or wrong, on the one hand, and, on the other, actually doing or refraining from doing it. This connection cannot, however, be a necessary or logical one, because we don't always do what we think is right. Yet the connection must be more than just an occasional coincidence. (This is quite a common kind of setting for a philosophical problem. Consider, for example, pain and its expression. There is no *necessary* connection between a groan and being in pain. Yet it isn't a coincidence that people who groan are in pain.) It certainly looks as if thinking that something is right or wrong *makes a difference* to how we behave. It doesn't, perhaps, make *all* the difference. But why should it, how can it, make any difference at all? How can knowledge or belief issue in action? Notice that putting the question this way round suggests that thinking and acting are separate, and that there is a problem about how they get together. We could equally well see a problem about how they ever come apart. Socrates saw the problem this way round. He wanted to know how sin is possible: how can knowledge ever *fail* to make a difference to how we behave?

The issue raised by determinism for moral philosophy, then, is just this: *are* we able to choose between alternative courses of action – as we must be, if we are to make any sense of good and evil? According to at least the stronger forms of determinism, we are not. The only thing we are able to do is the one thing we do in fact do; the alternatives, which at the time of action we think we are also able to do, we are in fact not able to do, and it is only an illusion that we are. But of course if at any time there is only one action that I am able or free to do, and I am not free to do anything else, then I am not *free* to do anything at all, including this thing that I do do. If I am falling off a cliff, it does not make much sense to say that I am free to hit the beach, when this is the only thing I can do. And if there is never anything that I am free to do, then there is nothing I can choose or decide to do, nothing I can claim credit or responsibility for, nothing which it can be said I ought or ought not to do. This is why it follows from determinism that moral concepts, while having a sort of meaning, do not apply to the actual world.

The principle operating here is 'Ought implies Can'. Spelt out, this means that if ever there is something I ought to do (if moral, or other value-concepts apply at all), then it must be possible for me to do it; and, we must add, possible for me to avoid doing it. We can see both points in the following example. Suppose I am a cruel jailer, and I say to a prisoner in his locked cell, 'You ought to leave'. This can only be a cruel jest, because if I sincerely thought he ought to leave, I must believe that he is able to leave. But now suppose the door is unlocked and the prisoner is dragged out unwillingly by several burly warders. Again, to say 'You ought to be leaving' can only be a cruel jest, because if I thought he ought to leave I must also think that he is able *not* to.

Now, there is no problem so long as we retain the common-sense assumption that in general there are *both* cases where we cannot choose between alternatives *and* cases where we can. But the determinist thesis is that there are *no* cases of the latter sort. How did people ever come to believe that determinism could be true? – that in fact we are never free to choose what to do? Well, it is a commonplace that determinism stems from science – from the outstanding successes of the sciences in the modern age in predicting and explaining more and more facts and phenomena, all based on a fundamental assumption about causality: that all events are such that they can be predicted from knowledge of their causes. This assumption has worked so well that the question is inevitably raised, why should human actions be exempt from the operation of causality? Even if it remains an assumption – and I shall show later that it cannot be proved – it still seems enormously plausible because of its success in other fields.

So here we have a confrontation between two metaphysical views: one based on science, and the other on common sense, in particular the common sense behind morality and the law, according to which of course a person is free to choose, and is correctly held responsible for what he does, because he was free to do otherwise (except in extreme conditions such as coercion or insanity).

Now although I said that determinism tends to be fostered by scientific thinking, science is not its only source. I am not thinking of cases where science itself implies an indeterminism, as quantum mechanics is said to do, but cases where there are deterministic tendencies outside science. Nor am I not thinking of the theological forerunner of determinism – the idea that, if an omniscient God knows that I shall do X, then I have no choice but to do X – for this was just as sophisticated in its day as materialistic determinism is today. No, I am thinking of deterministic

[21]

tendencies much nearer the common-sense level. One of these is expressed in the French saying 'Tout comprendre, c'est tout pardonner', which is meant to imply that we should be less inclined to blame wrongdoers, because if we understood enough there would be nothing left to blame: unfortunately it has a less desirable implication, that we should not praise people either, for exactly the same reason. Again, certain theories and practices of punishment have a strong undercurrent of determinism about them, and not only because they have been influenced by the deterministic thinking of modern psychologists: some of them are far too old for that. The Deterrent and the Reformative Theories were each advocated by Plato, and even then they were already foreshadowed in the Greek language itself, which has different words for punishment depending on whether it is retributive or corrective. Both the Deterrent and the Reformative Theories explicitly rely on an assumption that punishment (or, strictly speaking, remedial treatment in the case of the reformative view) will have specific effects on the criminal. In Deterrent theories, it is true, a certain amount of freedom and responsibility remains, because the criminal is supposed to think about his fate and his prospects, to choose between the evils of crime and punishment; but even this has disappeared in the vanguard of the reform movements, such as that led by Baroness Wootton who has been quoted as claiming that the distinction between prisons and hospitals ought to disappear. And of course this distinction, between penal and remedial institutions, just is the distinction between the voluntary offender and the sufferer from an unwanted disease. Samuel Butler's satire *Erewhon*, instead of abolishing the distinction, reverses it.

So much by way of introducing the issue. I now want to conduct a typical debate between antagonists supporting and attacking determinism, using certain standard moves and counter-moves. (Key propositions are numbered, and lettered either with D (for determinist) or F (for free will).)

(D)1 (*Universal Causation.*) Every event has a cause, and can be predicted and explained by reference to natural conditions over which human beings have no control.

(F)2(a) *The denial of 1.*

[22]

Let us leave the dialogue for a while and look at this important first stage: the determinist thesis and its rival. The first thing to note is that no philosophical thesis of any importance can be definitely proved or disproved, though of course there are other ways in which it can win out against its rivals – by being more intelligible, less paradoxical, involving fewer unsupported assumptions, or simply being closer to common sense. It does eventually turn out, I think, that the anti-determinist thesis, the thesis of freedom, though not provable, can be seen as more plausible, in these ways, than the determinist thesis. But let us first understand how it is, on the basis of strict logic, that neither thesis is open to proof or disproof. Let us take the simplest possible versions of the rival theses: *All events are caused* and *Some events are uncaused*. Compare them with propositions *of the same form* which *can* be proved, or disproved. 'All swans are white' cannot be proved, but it can be disproved, by the discovery of a non-white swan, which has in fact occurred. 'Some swans are not white', which is simply its contradictory, can therefore be proved, but not disproved. And 'Some swans are purple' like-wise cannot be disproved, and *can* be proved, even though it has not been and probably will not be. But the propositions about caused events behave quite differently from the ones about white swans. The reason why 'All events have causes' differs from 'All swans are white', so that it is not only not provable, but not even disprovable, is because it has a hidden structure. In logical jargon, it is doubly, or rather triply, quantified. It contains a 'some', and a second 'all' concealed in the term 'cause'. Roughly, to say 'All events are caused' is to say 'Every event is related to some other event in such a way that whenever an event of the second kind occurs, an event of the first kind occurs'. This cannot be proved, for the same reason as 'All swans are white'. But it cannot even be disproved, because of the 'some' component in the expansion just given, which behaves like 'Some swan is purple' and is not disprovable. To put the matter more informally: we know that the discovery of a non-white swan can, and indeed did, disprove the proposition that all swans are white; but there is no such thing as the discovery of an uncaused event to disprove the proposition that all events are caused. This is because the non-white swan is a definite datum and quite final; but the uncaused event is not. For in the case of any alleged uncaused event it is always possible to re-examine the situation and find that there is, or might be, a cause after all. Clearly it would be insane for the white-swan theorist to say, when confronted with the Australian bird, 'Hold on, I'm sure that if we examine this swan more carefully we shall find that it is white after all'; yet it is not merely not insane, but positively appropriate, for an investigator confronted with an unpredicted anomaly to claim that further research will explain it and enable it to be predicted next time.

All this applies equally to the counter-thesis of 'freedom'. So far, then, we have stalemate. But perhaps the freedom thesis can get the advantage if, in addition to a bare denial of 1, it goes on to assert something positive about the nature of human action. So let it say something like

> (F)2(b) (*The 'will' thesis*) In addition to external, natural, factors, there is a special internal factor, usually called the will, which is beyond the reach of science, and of which we have immediate awareness in our experience of choice, decision, and purposive action.

But the Determinist has a ready answer to this:

> (D)3 *The so-called 'will' is just one of those unwanted fictions* (like conscience, as on p.10) invented as a pseudo-explanatory device to account for the common-sense distinction between voluntary and involuntary action. As such it is a very poor device and easily refuted by the following argument. If an action is voluntary when it is preceded by an act of will, and not otherwise, is this act of will itself voluntary, or is it involuntary? If it is involuntary, then the action as a whole is involuntary after all. But if it is voluntary, this can only be explained by postulating a further act of will, which leads to a vicious infinite regress. As to the claim that acts of will are revealed in experience, this is merely specious. What we experience *is* choice, decisions, and so on.

A new attack on 1 and 3 seizes on the idea of predicting human actions, as opposed to events.

> (F)4 (*Human Unpredictability*) Predictions about human ac-

tions can always be frustrated. This is a power peculiar to human beings. Nature cannot frustrate our predictions (except in an obviously metaphorical sense), but man always can. If someone predicts that I will vote Labour, I can always prove him wrong, and if I am a cussed sort of chap I probably will.

(D)5 (*Denial of* 4) Predicting something is itself an event. This event can be causally related to the behaviour one is predicting, for instance by the person concerned coming to hear of it. (Communication is itself a form of causal interaction.) So a prediction will have its own effects, and these must be taken into account in a reliable prediction. (My reference to being a 'cussed chap' was precisely to a prediction's own effects.)

This exchange can continue. Call the person who makes the initial prediction the prediction-maker, and the agent who tries to frustrate the prediction, the prediction-breaker. Then the prediction-maker will make a series of more and more refined predictions, each taking account of the effect on the prediction-breaker of the latest prediction. On the face of it, it looks as if the prediction-breaker will just win, because he is always one step ahead. But if the prediction-maker keeps his prediction secret, *he* will win!

(D/F)6 (*The Compatibility Thesis*) Determinism and Freedom are not incompatible. This is a new and more explicitly philosophical development. The possibility or otherwise of exact prediction is irrelevant, for two reasons. Firstly, morality does *not* require unpredictability, but rather the reverse. Secondly, predictability is *not* incompatible with freedom.

So far from requiring unpredictability, morality requires just the opposite. A person whose actions really were unpredictable, so that we could never know how he would act in any kind of situation, would be a person of no character, and therefore of no moral character. None of the moral concepts of reliability, trustworthiness or responsibility could apply to him. So it looks as if morality actually requires at least some form of determinism.

If morality requires predictability, then predictability cannot be destructive of freedom. Why did it ever seem so? The mistake was to equate predictability with inevitability. Certainly, if whatever is predictable is unavoidable, it will be a case of unfreedom. But it is true that if something is predictable, it is unavoidable? No; for this is to say that, if something is going to happen, it is *necessarily* going to happen, that nothing can stop it. But it is (usually) false that if something will happen, it will necessarily happen. This can only be the case if the prediction is necessarily true, and so infallible. Some predictions, to be sure, *are* necessarily true, such as the prediction made on Thursday that tomorrow will be Friday. But this is a trivial consequence of the calendar. Predictions of events are not like that. Aristotle got into a tizzy about the famous sea battle tomorrow. It seemed that, since every proposition is either true or false, the proposition that there will be a sea battle tomorrow is, today, either true, or else it is false; so either the sea battle is bound to happen, or it cannot possibly happen; so whether it happens or not seems to be already decided by pure logic, and not something that depends on the decisions of the admirals. (This is Fatalism, which is also called Logical Determinism.) But of course this is nonsense. It puts the relation between the event predicted and the prediction of the event precisely the wrong way round. Whether the event occurs or not is what determines whether the prediction is true or false. It's not that a true prediction somehow forces the predicted event to come about.

Another way of putting this is to say that causes do not compel. A cause (and we are supposing that predictions are based on causal knowledge) explains what has happened, and also what will happen, but it does not (usually) *compel* what will happen to happen. In the field of human action very few causes are coercive, though some are, like the prison walls of my earlier example, which literally force me to stay in my cell, or the brute strength of the warders who compel me to leave. But the great majority of cases where we speak of being 'forced' to do something are not like this. Even when I am 'forced' by the gunman to hand over the cash, I still have other alternatives open to me, though I will probably not choose them. I still incur responsibility, if not blame. On this view about causes, the name 'determinism' is misleading, for it is fully consistent with freedom. Doesn't freedom mean doing what I want, or what I have good reasons for doing? As Mill put it, 'We may be free, and yet another may have reason to be perfectly certain what use we shall make of our freedom.'⁶

We now come to the final counter-attack by the thoroughgoing determinist.

(D)7 (*Ideal Determinism*) The attempt to reconcile determinism and freedom, just considered, relied on the common-sense view that predictions of human behaviour are as a matter of fact not totally reliable, they can often turn out to be false. But the determinist who is really worth his salt is not likely to argue from the present imperfect state of the human sciences, but from what he claims they could in principle be developed into. A really full explanation of any human action would, it is claimed, show that what happened really was inevitable; and a really complete set of data on which to base such a prediction really would leave no room for falsification. So responsibility and choice really are excluded, not by our present working knowledge of human affairs, but by our belief in a fully deterministic world. So it will not do to say that freedom is doing what you want, because in a fully deterministic world your wants, which determine what you do, are themselves determined.

(F)8 (*Reason and Freedom*) This final counter-move can only be met by looking into the idea of doing what you want, and, finally of having a good reason for acting. Take wanting first. The determinist attacks this by arguing that wants are themselves what determine your actions. He explains away the supposed freedom of doing X, when you could have done Y instead, by saying that all this means is that you *would* have done Y instead, *if* you had wanted to. Against this, however, we can make a point which Kant made: that it is *not* always true that my wants determine my actions, so that I would necessarily have done Y if I had wanted to. Sometimes at least I *could* have done Y even if I had not wanted to: for it is possible to act contrary to our wants. This happens, if not always, at least on many occasions when I have a good reason for not doing what I want to do. (I can have a very good reason for not drinking another pint, which I desire, and I can succeed in not drinking.) Admittedly the fact that I want to do something is always itself a reason for doing it, but there may be, and often are, better reasons for my not doing it. Wants can be outweighed by other reasons. So the case for freedom rests ultimately on the idea of acting for reasons.

So – finally – can *reason* be taken as determining our actions and as being themselves determined? The determinist *can* try to say about reasons what he said about wants. He can say that doing what you have good reasons to choose to do is still not freedom, because what *appears* to you to be a good or bad reason is itself conditioned by your total psychological response to the situation as it presents itself to you.

This cannot be fully answered without a detailed discussion of what it is to act for reasons – a difficult issue on which philosophers are by no means agreed. I shall give only a hint of a solution, which is to say: if what we are now said to be 'determined' by are *reasons*, what difference remains to contrast with 'freedom'? Surely there is now no opposition whatever between them. Descartes described the situation very well in *Meditation IV* when he spoke of acting freely 'because a great illumination of the understanding was followed by a great inclination of the will'. In other words, determination by reasons is just a case of that very basic idea of doing what you want – following your inclinations. True, I have criticised this idea as inadequate, because I don't *have* to do what I want; I can be even more free in acting contrary to my wants. But this will only be true where I sacrifice some crude, simple, or short-term want in favour of some more considered, or long-term, goal; or some moral obligation. And of course the long-term goal, such as achieving happiness, or living up to certain moral standards, are things I want. Of course they differ from ordinary short-term desires, or cravings. They involve reflection on what is worth having in the long run, for my future self, or for other people. They are typically *rational* wants. And surely in acting according to *these* wants, wishes or aspirations, I cannot be other than acting freely.

Just to clinch the matter – to show that the 'freedom' thesis is indeed more intelligible, more inescapable, than any determinist thesis which rejects free will (and, as we have seen, not all versions do, in the case of compatibilism) – let us reflect on what is involved in treating each other as persons, as fellow human beings. Now there are ways in which we sometimes fail to do this; sometimes quite properly, as in the case of a surgeon making an incision, sometimes very unproperly, as in the case of torturing, or brainwashing. Notice that at these sub-personal levels it is quite in order to think deterministically: the human being is an object to be manipulated, which certainly implies a thoroughly causal relationship. But when we treat each other as persons, we cannot avoid the vocabulary of *action*, of people *doing* things, and that already carries with it the notions of choice and responsibility. We *can* avoid talking in this vocabulary, no doubt, but the cost is unimaginably high.

Finally, the last nail in the coffin of (hard) determinism is this. We turn from actions in the ordinary, bodily, sense, to acts of saying, thinking and believing things. If we are to be free to act, we must be free to think and believe, since our thoughts 'determine' our actions. And conversely, if our acts of thinking or forming beliefs must be free, then at least some of our actions must be. But what we believe to be true, we believe because of good reasons. Now if (hard) determinism is true, these are only *causes* of our beliefs, not reasons. So if determinism is true, there is no reason to believe that it is.

Determinism and propaganda

Before we leave the issue of determinism and freedom, I want to show that it is by no means a purely theoretical issue: here is an area where philosophy can have a practical effect, even if only a remedial one. First, we are all familiar with the rhetoric of confrontation in such matters as industrial disputes, or terrorist activities, whereby people who are doing harm, such as going on strike or engaging in violence, claim that they are 'forced' to act in these ways by other people who will not accede to their demands.

This is pernicious cant, but highly effective. It exploits the idea, true in itself, that if person A forces person B to do X, where X is something harmful, then two things follow: first, person B is not, after all, to be blamed for X (because he was not free), and, second, that person A *is* to be blamed (because it was he who initiated the harm). So the terrorist's guilt is not only shrugged off, but actually transferred to the victim's government. What is perniciously false here is the refusal to distinguish between: 'Person A's acts causally affect person B's', and: 'Person A *forces* person B to act'. To point out, as we have done, that causes are not (normally, and certainly not in these cases) coercive, is to demolish this rhetoric.

Here is another example, which illustrates both some points about determinism and freedom, and some points about emotivism, which I shall be dealing with later. The example shows how the idea of psychological determinism can be exploited for political purposes by unscrupulous politicians. I once read in an American newspaper a speech by J. Edgar Hoover, who was then director of the FBI; the context was a student demonstration in San Francisco:

> The successful Communist exploitation and manipulation of youth and student groups throughout the world today are a major challenge which free world forces must meet and defeat. Recent world events clearly reveal that world Communism has launched a massive campaign to capture and manoeuvre youth and student groups. The vigour and vitality of such groups constitute an explosive force of immense proportions. Channelled into proper outlets, this force can accomplish immeasurable good for a peace-loving world. Manipulated into destructive action, this force can create chaos.

Notice first the contrast between 'channelling' and 'manipulating'. Channelling seems to be a good, or at least neutral, thing, while manipulating, along with capturing and manoeuvring, seem to be a bad thing. But surely, we may ask, these are just the same thing with different names. Now the same thing can't be both good and bad, even if the different names make it seem so. Anticipating somewhat, and diagnosing a certain emotional bias in the speaker, we might suspect that there is indeed some process that the speaker approves of when it is applied by the people he approves of, but disapprove of when the same process is applied by people he disapproves of, and that he uses words with different overtones accordingly. In fact *all* the operative words in the passage turn out to be like this: they are not so much descriptive of fact, as expressive of attitudes towards the facts. Let us re-write part of the message, distinguishing explicitly between words descriptive of fact, and words which purport to be descriptive, but in reality only express different attitudes, of favour or disfavour, depending on the speaker's political commitment.

The successful $\begin{array}{c}\text{Communist } \textit{exploitation}\\\text{Christian } \textit{enlistment}\end{array}$ of youth groups is a

major $\begin{array}{c}\textit{challenge}\\\textit{achievement}\end{array}$ which $\begin{array}{cc}\textit{free} & \text{Christian}\\\textit{unfree} & \text{Communist}\end{array}$ world forces. . . .

Now we have a recipe for the anti-Communist political activist: choose the upper word if you are talking about Communists doing things to youth groups, choose the lower word if you are talking about Christians doing the same things. A different recipe for the Communist political activist . . .

So far, this has been just a foretaste of a discussion of Emotivism. But we can see that freedom and unfreedom, which have their own very powerful emotive associations, favourable and unfavourable, are themselves among the key words, which we can tabulate as follows:

channelling	manipulating, capturing, manoeuvring
guiding	forcing
teaching	indoctrinating
preaching	brainwashing
demonstrating	rioting
enlisting	exploiting
free	*unfree*

Now if good things are happening, and they are happening to good people (in this case, American students), these young people can be allowed to be responsible for the good things,

[31]

because they freely embrace them; and we use vocabulary from the left-hand column. But if bad things are happening, yet because the same good people are involved, they must have their responsibility somehow switched off. And nothing is easier; all it takes is a switch of vocabulary. The responsibility is not merely switched off, but switched across from the young people to their manipulators in the right-hand column, who thus come to incur a *double* odium: not only are they responsible for the evil doings, but they are also culpable for diminishing the freedom of their innocent victims.

So perhaps philosophy can be of some practical use. Just as a training in logic can help to expose fallacies in thinking, so even a limited amount of conceptual analysis can help to expose rhetorical duplicity. As R.M. Hare has well said, 'If a person is able to distinguish genuine facts from those "facts" which are really concealed evaluations . . . then the propagandist will have little power over him. To arm people in this way against propaganda is the function of moral philosophy.'[7] I can hardly go as far as '*the* function', but certainly this can be one of its benefits.

CHAPTER III

Naturalism and intuitionism

Having defused the determinist threat to the applicability of value-judgments, we may now return to the question of the nature and status of values. The question 'What are (moral) values?' is certainly a meta-ethical question, but it cannot be answered in anything like that simple form. It must be broken down into something more manageable; perhaps 'what are (moral) value-judgments?' But even this formula conceals the enormous variety of phenomena that need to be taken account of. Consider the following list of items, all of which are clearly at the heart of morality.

A 1 Deciding that I ought to do X rather than Y (in this and the next two items X and Y refer to specific acts, and 'ought' is understood to have moral force rather than prudential or technical).

2 Advising you that you ought to do X . . .

3 Commenting on her that she ought to do X . . ., or ought to have done X.

4 Feeling remorse for not having done X . . .

5 Feeling disapproval for her not doing X . . .

B 6 Expressing a general moral view (such as in discussing issues like abortion, pacifism, etc.)

7 Following a general rule or principle.

C 8 Being a Utilitarian (in this and the next item the label stands for some ultimate and pervasive moral position).

9 Being a Nazi; Christian; or Humanist.

These items vary in several dimensions. They range from specific acts (A) to very general moral standpoints (C). They may refer to the future (1,2) or the past (4,5) or timelessly (B, C). They may relate to the speaker (1,4), the person addressed (2), a third person (3,5), or everyone (B, C). They may be decisions, spoken judgments, unspoken thoughts, feelings, principles, or a whole way of life.

Now it seems reasonable to think that all the items on the list, despite their enormous variety, have something in common, which distinguishes the judgments among them from statements of ordinary matters of fact, and also distinguishes all the items from similar items in other fields of value, such as aesthetics, prudence, or religion. *The task of meta-ethics is to discover what that something is.*

We can also say that the central question of meta-ethics is simply to find what distinguishes the moral from the non-moral. Care is needed here, because the term 'moral' does not have a simple opposite. It has at least three contrasting terms. One is, of course, 'immoral', but this is obviously itself a moral term. Another is 'amoral', but even this is a term of the moral vocabulary, since to say that someone is an amoral person is to say that he is a person who does not care for morality, or who has, or professes to have, no moral principles. Only the term 'non-moral', as distinct from these others, can be used at the meta-ethical level. There is an exact analogy with religion here. The term 'theistic' also has three contrasts, not one. 'Atheist' is certainly a term of theology; and so is 'agnostic', because, again, to say that someone is a religious agnostic is to say that he is a person who does not care to form beliefs, or who has, or professes to have, no beliefs either way. Only the term 'non-theistic' could be used at the level of philosophy of religion, or meta-religious enquiry, an enquiry about what religious phenomena have distinctively in common.

When I stated the task of meta-ethics two paragraphs back (italics), I began by picking out those items in the list which could be regarded as *judgments*. (This is a very natural move, but as we shall see it can be questioned.) Let us return to the Longford obscenity test in Chapter 1 (p.17). In the quotation there was a contrast between 'judgments of value' which were said not to admit of an 'empirical test', and judgments which do – these being, usually, judgments of fact. Facts, especially facts which are empirically testable or observable, are unquestionably *objective*. (Science is the very paradigm of what is purely objective.) Values, on the other hand, are, notoriously, not *unquestionably* objective; we were then discussing that very question. The problem is particularly acute when we bring facts and values together in the very same context, instead of just relegating facts to science and values to ethics, art and religion. Most of the time we *can* keep our science and ethics apart, though not always, as in the case of weapons research or animal experiments. And facts and values seem to collide most disagreeably when we are conscious of our own moral failure, as in the confession of St Paul: 'The good that I would do, I do not; but the evil which I would not, that I do.' But quite generally there is an all too obvious contrast between the good that ought to be the case, and the evil that ought not to be the case, but is.

However, many philosophers have gone on thinking that values must be some sort of facts, and we must look at certain theories of this kind, and see how and why even the most plausible ones come to grief. Let us start by distinguishing between 'ordinary' facts and extra-ordinary ones. Ordinary facts will be facts which are established by scientific methods and the common-sense methods from which science has developed. 'Empirical' roughly covers these methods. The extra-ordinary facts will be facts which can only be established, if at all, by non-scientific methods, such as revelation, mystical experience, astrology, intuition, and so on. Now the very simplest theory (in a certain sense) about moral facts will be the theory that moral judgments are like ordinary factual statements except that they are about *extra*-ordinary facts instead of ordinary ones. Such a theory was held by Plato, and has been held by Intuitionists. We shall have to examine it in some detail later, but for the moment let me just say that, although it is the *simplest* theory, it is utterly unplausible. (John Mackie has used 'the argument from queer-ness' in rejecting it.) So we shall take first the next simplest type of theory: Naturalism. Naturalism, or at least the classical form of it, takes its character from a certain pervasive tendency in modern British philosophy, namely Empiricism. There is a certain economy-drive, sometimes called Occam's Razor, according to which we are not to allow into our world-picture any 'facts' of an extravagantly non-scientific sort, such as Platonic or intuitionistic values would have to be. Instead, values are indeed facts of a certain sort, but they are not facts of an extra-ordinary sort. Or rather their peculiarity is only that we are not perfectly familiar with the geographical details. It is rather like the fact of being an electrical conductor. We all know that copper is an electrical conductor and rubber is not, but very few of us know what the actual facts are which *constitute* being an electrical conductor. These are quite complicated facts about electron shells – the geography of the copper atom. Just so, according to the ethical naturalist, we all know that torturing people is wrong and helping the sick is good, but few of us know what are the facts about torturing people or helping the sick which *make* them wrong, or good. A naturalist theory claims to tell us what these facts are.

Before we look at some examples of naturalistic theories, we must consider more exactly what they are theories *about*. What are the data they are trying to explain? It won't do to say 'values', because values are not rock-bottom data: they are abstractions (though not for that reason unreal: gravity and electricity are abstractions, but certainly not unreal). The data will be, not values, but the *expressions* of values in our ordinary day-to-day lives – what actually goes on when we think and feel. But what does go on? The trouble is that a great variety of things go on – there are enormously many ways in which values are expressed. I have already listed some on p.33. There are choices, decisions, resolutions. Coming nearer to language, there are expressive gestures like frowns and raised eyebrows. In language there are many different constructions and grammatical forms: indicatives (torturing is wrong), imperatives (don't break your promise); interrogatives (what right have you to . . . ?); expletives (how awful!) and so on. Now why do we tend to pick *judgments* out of the list? Well, any theory has to simplify; it cannot absorb a whole mass of data in one go. So we find that a selection is always made from all the available data; a certain sort of datum is taken as typical or basic; the idea being that if you can explain those data, the others will be explained in due course. Now since philosophers are so much concerned with concepts and meanings, and these seem to figure most prominently in *statements*, it isn't surprising to find that the kind of moral datum which gets selected as the most typical or basic one is the statement, or what looks like a statement because it has the same grammatical form – the indicative. This is called a value-judgment. Later on we shall see what happens when a different selection is made, such as the imperative.

So, we are talking about value-judgments, and the important thing about them is that they generally have the same form as ordinary factual statements. Just as we say 'Jones is ten stone in weight', so we say 'Jones is a good man' or 'a villain'. Just as we say 'Copper is conductive', so we say 'torturing is evil'. We are concerned with (what appear to be) *statements* assigning (what appear to be) *properties* – moral properties – to persons, or actions. And we want to know exactly what sort of properties these are. Now if we had a theory which says that these rather mysterious properties (goodness, wrongness) are really equivalent to some quite unmysterious properties, we should have an *explanation*. An explanation is what reduces the unfamiliar to the familiar.

Note that word 'reducing'. Theories are often described as *reductionist*, especially philosophical theories. Since naturalism, and another theory to be discussed later, emotivism, are both cases of reductionist theories in ethics, I'll say a bit more about how a theory can try to 'reduce' one thing to another. (Some philosophers object to the idea at the outset: G.E. Moore quotes with approval Butler's dictum 'Everything is what it is, and not another thing'.)

What, then, is a reductionist theory, and what can be attractive about it? There are two kinds of reductionism, the second much more drastic than the first. The first, less drastic, kind is a view which holds that a whole class of statements about some class of

[37]

entities can be replaced by (because they really mean the same as) a different class of statements about some (apparently) different class of entities. (Of course, if this is to be a rewarding exercise, the second class of entities will have to be more familiar, or less problematic, than the first.) For example, there are reductionist theories of psychology: some claim that the whole class of statements about experiences, feelings, and consciousness can be replaced by statements about the behaviour of bodies. Others claim that these psychological statements can be replaced with statements about neuro-physiological events. So psychology is 'reduced' to behaviour, or to neuro-physiology; minds are 'nothing but' complex movements of bodies, or complex interactions of neurones. (Reductionism has been called 'nothing-buttery'.)

The second, more drastic, kind of reductionism does not replace one set of statements with another set of statements which, being statements, will still be true or false, but claims that the original statements are not really statements at all, and can only be replaced by, or reduced to, something which is not true or false, but something more like an exclamation, or an expression of a need, drive or emotion. An example of this would be a certain kind of reductionist theory of religion on the lines of Karl Marx's celebrated dictum about the opiate of the people: statements about a god are not merely not statements about a god, they are not statements about anything whatever, but are a mere expression of a human need for security, irresponsibility, or whatever. Both types of reductionist theories occur in ethics. Naturalism is of the first kind, emotivism of the second. Naturalism takes seriously what appear to be moral statements; emotivism takes seriously other items in the list, such as the frowns and raised eyebrows.

An early example of a reductionist theory in ethics, a form of naturalism, can be seen in the 'theory' advanced by a character in Plato's dialogue *The Republic*, Thrasymachus. Justice, or doing right, is the topic; how can it be defined? Quite simply, says Thrasymachus: it is the interest of the stronger. Expanded slightly, this turns out to mean that justice is, means, doing what you are told by the authorities; and the authorities issue their orders, lay down their laws, in accordance with what is most profitable to themselves. We can leave out this bit, about the motivation of rulers, which belongs to political theory and psychology, and concentrate on the first bit: justice means doing what you are told by the authorities. This is a reductionist theory because it holds that whenever we talk about justice we could always talk instead about what we are required to do by the powers that be. And it is *reductionist* because it leaves or rules out such problematic ideas normally associated with justice as the idea of something fixed, eternal, absolute, independent of particular persons such as rulers. But it is a reductionist theory of the first kind because there is still room for truth and falsity in it. (There are also traces of the more drastic second kind, which we shall note later.)

A naturalist theory, then, is going to deal with moral judgments, that is, utterances of the form 'X is right' or 'wrong', 'Y is good' or 'evil', and it is going to do three things:

(1) Because it is a reductionist theory, it is going to say that the supposed properties of being right or wrong, good or evil, are really equivalent to some other properties. The attraction of this is that the other properties are (a) more familiar, and (b), hopefully, such that we can more easily verify whether they are there or not, so that moral questions, so notoriously difficult to settle, will become more easily settlable.

(2) Because it is a naturalist theory, the properties in question are going to be those open to detection by the natural sciences, or their common-sense counterparts.

(3) Because it is a *particular* naturalist theory, as opposed to several others, it will identify one particular *sort* of property.

To sum up so far: moral judgments are notoriously problematic. According to some philosophers (such as the Logical Positivists) they are actually meaningless unless we can show how to verify them. Naturalist theories offer to rescue ethics from perpetual uncertainty, or even meaninglessness, by offering substitute statements which we know how to verify, and claiming that they are equivalent to the original moral judgments. It is not easy to find out whether something is good or bad; it is very easy to find out whether something is yellow or square. If we could only discover some property or other which was really equivalent to goodness, but which was checkable in the sort of way that yellowness and squareness are, then a reductionist theory of the first kind will hold, and moral judgments will be decidable, capable of being true or false. If such a property can *not* be found, then a reductionist theory of the second, destructive, kind is available, and moral judgments will become meaningless, or, at best, capable of some inferior kind of meaning, not that connected with saying what is true or false. Naturalism is the attempt to find such a property; emotivism is one result of failing to find it.

Before examining some specimen naturalist theories, we must clear up a preliminary difficulty about the two pairs of terms 'right/wrong' and 'good/bad' (or 'good/evil') which I have been using so far more or less interchangeably. It is a convenience to use the terms which have been commonly thought to be the key terms in moral judgments – just as the naturalists select from the variety of moral phenomena those that look most like statements, so they select from the terms occurring in these statements those that seem to refer most directly to the supposed moral properties: the right and the good. But they are not interchangeable. 'Right' and 'wrong' apply primarily to actions. 'Good' and 'bad' or 'evil' apply much more widely, to states of affairs, to people, characters, and motives. A good action is not the same as a right action. There are complex relations and dependencies between the good and the right (and their opposites). A wrong action may be one that produces harm. A good man is one who tends to do right actions because they are right. A good action is one done with a good motive, or such as a good man would do. And so on. I mention this point here because naturalist theories may differ according to whether the theory applies primarily to the right, or to the good. In the list below, the appropriate term will have to be supplied.[8]

According to the following four naturalistic theories, then, to say that something is M (where 'M' is one of the terms just discussed) means that it is productive of, conducive to, or consists of

    (1) the pleasure of the agent (Egoistic Hedonism)
    (2) the pleasure of the recipient (Altruistic Hedonism)
    (3) the pleasure of most people (Utilitarianism)
    (4) the survival of the species (Evolutionism)

[40]

These four, unlike the next four, may be regarded as *consequentialist* theories. The property to which M is reduced is that of having a certain consequence in the world which is open to empirical investigation. Notice that the first three theories are all forms of hedonism, and it is a simple matter of fact whether or not someone is pleased. (3) of course involves practical difficulties in fact-finding, but that is not a relevant objection. The same applies to (4), where it would indeed be a difficult matter to establish survival value in a particular case, but this again is not the point. The next four theories may be classed together as *legislative*: to say that something is M is to say that it is willed, approved, or sanctioned by

(5) the speaker (Private Subjectivism)
(6) most people (Public Subjectivism)
(7) an authority (Authoritarian Subjectivism)
(8) God (Theological Ethics)

One might be surprised to find the word 'subjectivism' here. Since naturalist theories are supposed to be thoroughly objectivist, how can they be subjectivist as well? The answer is that even facts about me are facts. If I dislike something, that is just as much a fact about me as any other. Now *if* 'X is wrong' did mean 'X is disliked by me', that would be an objectivist theory. Of course it is obviously false, because *you* may not dislike X, in which case X will be both right and wrong, a contradiction. Other forms of subjectivism, however, such as (6) and (7), are not so obviously wrong. A special difficulty arises over (8), a very important theory which we shall discuss in its own right later. The difficulty here is to see how (8) can be classed as a naturalist theory. Part of the answer is that it is just convenient, for the purpose of classifying ethical theories, to include a supernatural property with natural ones. But what about the emphasis on the empirical? We certainly do not find out the will of God by empirical investigation. The best I can do to justify including this non-empirical property is to point out that it shares with the empirical properties the negative feature of being ascertainable, in principle, independently of any moral judgment. (This will have to be questioned, however, in Chapter VIII.)

We come now to the objections to naturalism. There are three, plus one to be dealt with later. All three are variants of what has been called the 'Naturalistic Fallacy' argument, but I shall not give this argument in its original version as propounded by G.E. Moore,[9] which has given rise to endless controversy. Remember that we are concerned with a type of theory which holds that 'this is M' means 'this is N', where 'M' is a supposed moral property and 'N' a 'natural' property as described above.

The first objection may be called *changing the subject*. (This is the substance of Butler's dictum, p.37.) Consider a typical moral dispute. (The facts of moral controversy, though not in my list of moral phenomena, except perhaps by implication, are in fact very important evidence for the plausibility of an ethical theory. No theory can stand if it has as a consequence that moral disputes are not really disputes.) Suppose A says 'Capital punishment is always wrong', and B says, 'No; it is justified when . . . ', and A continues to insist 'Never'. Suppose B says 'Most people do in fact approve' or 'The human race would not have survived without it'. Now according to the relevant version of naturalism, B would be saying just the same thing that he said before. But surely A is entitled to object, 'So what? Please don't change the subject!' In other words, when ethical properties are reduced to some other properties, we are just talking about the wrong thing.

The next version is the 'open question' argument. Even if it *could* be established beyond doubt that a certain action does have the property N, that doesn't settle the moral question. It is always possible to reply 'I agree that this would give more pleasure to more people than anything else would, but it would still be wrong.' Or, to take the majority subjectivism version, it must be possible to think that people, even most people, are wrong; that their views are open to criticism. (Even in my own case, it must be *possible* for me to be wrong.)

The third version is Hume's Law (see p.4), which is commonly paraphrased as: it is impossible to derive *ought* from *is*; or, no statement of fact by itself implies any judgment of value. In terms of logic, no conclusion can be validly drawn if it contains material not in the premisses. But a value-judgment contains a value element and therefore cannot be derived from premisses which contain only matters of (natural) fact. But if M cannot be derived from N, they certainly cannot be equivalent; so naturalism fails.

Assuming, as I shall, that these objections are conclusive, how do we react? Philosophers have reacted in different ways. Two extreme reactions are worth noting. The first is to make moral properties not natural, but 'non-natural'. And the second is to deny that they are properties of any kind. We start with the first. This is called non-naturalism and is associated with G.E. Moore and intuitionism. It is an attractively simple view, but open to overwhelming objections. It holds that, since the property of being good or right cannot be identified with any other sort of property, then it can only be identified with itself; that is, there just is this property of goodness, which belongs to some actions or states and not to others, just as there is the property (to use Moore's example) of being yellow, which belongs to things like lemons but not to tomatoes. Also like yellow, it is simple and unanalysable. But unlike yellow, of course it is not open to observation. We have to invoke special, non-natural powers of detection. The technical term for this kind of power or faculty is intuition; hence the theory's name. Nor is this type of theory specially designed for ethics; it has been popular in aesthetics too. Compare this remark by C.E.M. Joad: 'Beauty is directly apprehended by the mind in just the same way that shape is directly apprehended.'[10]

Intuitionism is, of course a – indeed the – non-reductionist theory. Superficially it has a certain appeal. It avoids all versions of the Naturalistic Fallacy (not surprisingly, since it was designed to do so). More positively, it fits in well with much of our experience and with much of what we tend to say about the phenomena of the moral life. We are inclined to talk about people of great moral discernment, or of people who are morally insensitive or even blind. We also speak of people having intense moral convictions, of *knowing* what they ought to, even when, and perhaps especially when, they are unable to give specific reasons, or to quote any general moral propositions to back up their convictions. Even more significantly, these convictions do seem to refer to something outside of, and independent of, the persons who have them; they do *not* seem to be just a matter of what people want or don't want, or personally approve or disapprove;

indeed they very often conflict with what they want ('I'd like to, but I can't'). Again, to bring in the analogy with 'ordinary' factual knowledge, these convictions do seem to impose themselves on us in much the same way as convictions about the nature of things; when I become convinced about such things as the enormous size of the sun, or the vast distance of the stars, I am convinced at the same time that these are matters utterly external to me, in no possible sense emanations or projections of my own being. (Quite the reverse; my own being seems to shrink into absolute insignificance in relation to these vast facts.) And similarly, my convictions about what I must do or avoid, how I must or must not direct my life, very often seem to come in much the same way, as things wholly external to me, and certainly not generated from within.

Yet despite this considerable appeal, the *theory* of intuitionism runs into very great difficulties. We must remember that we are not talking about the phenomena themselves – no harm will be done in using the word 'intuition' to describe some of the experiences just mentioned – but about a theory which purports to explain and systematise these phenomena, and, in addition, to pass the tests for a satisfactory theory. And if it turns out that intuitionism, as a theory, cannot pass these tests, then the phenomena will have to be explained by some other theory which can; for they certainly *are* facts. Now what are the tests which intuitionism fails?

(1) The first and most obvious trouble is that the theory requires us to believe in the existence, and detectability, of very peculiar properties; that such things as goodness and rightness are just out there, somehow attaching to things and waiting to be detected by our moral sensors. This is the substance of Mackie's Argument from Queerness, and needs no elaboration. But there are several other objections which are worth following up, since they will lead us to a set of tests which we can apply to any proposed ethical theory.

(2) The theory speaks of *knowledge*, yet leaves no room for *belief*. Now in all other cases of attaining knowledge, knowledge seems to lie at the end of a series which starts with ignorance, doubt, and uncertainty, moves through belief of various degrees, and

finally becomes knowledge. Yet intuitive knowledge seems to be an all-or-nothing affair. We are either totally illuminated, or totally benighted, depending on whether an intuition has occurred, or not. There can be no room for a half-intuition. Similarly there is no room in the theory for evidence, or grounds of belief.

(3) How do we know when an intuition has occurred? People certainly make judgments about what is right or wrong, but however sincerely they make them, they often contradict each other, and change their own minds; all these judgments seem to arise in much the same way, yet only some of them can arise from intuitions, because intuitions are by definition true; but how can we possibly tell which are intuitions and which are not? Certainly not by inspection, since the false ones – or rather those which turn out not to have been intuitions – will be indistinguishable from true or genuine ones.

(4) Consequently, intuitionism will be unable to give a satisfactory account of the phenomenon of moral controversy. One of the intuitionist writers, H.A. Prichard, tries to meet this objection as follows:

(a) The appreciation of an obligation is only possible for a developed moral being, and different degrees of moral development are possible. (b) The failure to recognise some particular obligation is usually due to the fact that, owing to a lack of thoughtfulness, the preliminaries to recognition are incomplete. (c) I admit that, owing to a lack of thoughtfulness, even the best men are blind to many of their obligations.[11]

The short answer to this is, I take it, this: just try telling one (or both) of the participants in a moral debate that he must be either immature or thoughtless.

(5) Another thing that intuitionism conspicuously leaves out is the public dimension of morality. Morality is not *only* a matter of 'appreciating' our own obligations. We also have to judge others. When I say we 'have' to, I don't of course mean that it is incumbent on each of us to go around expressing adverse, or even favourable, criticism on everybody else. It is that we are necessarily committed to judgments on others, though not of course to uttering those judgments. The point is that morality,

[45]

even my morality, is not about any particular person, whether me or anyone else. In judging the morality of an action, it makes no difference whose action it is. This is the feature of morality which we shall later meet under the heading of universality. Morality requires an impersonal standpoint. But intuitions, being supposedly private acts, are as defective as conscience in this report. I have already criticised conscience as vacuous. Another criticism is that it is egocentric. My conscience is supposed to tell me what to do, but I am not expected to hear it telling me what you or she should do. It is like what Wittgenstein says of God: ' "You can't hear God when he speaks to someone else, only when he speaks to you" – that is a grammatical remark.'[12]

(6) Finally, intuitionism totally fails to account for a feature of morality that I have not yet mentioned. This is an objection that applies to naturalism as well (it is the fourth objection to be added to the three on p.42). It applies to all theories which assume that moral terms stand for properties – whether natural or non-natural – all theories which hold that a moral judgment of the form 'this is right' or 'good' literally describes some action as having some property to be discovered by observation, intuition, or any other mode there may be of ascertaining a truth. Now what is ignored by all these theories is what may be called the *motivational force* of the words in question. An essential part of the meaning of these words is that if I think of something as good, I must *necessarily* be favourably disposed towards getting, pursuing, or keeping it; I must be seeking or striving towards its realization or preservation; and anything I believe to be wrong, I must *necessarily* have an aversion to, a repugnance which must affect (even though it may not finally determine) my conduct. This motivational function of moral words, or action-guiding function, has to be ignored by naturalist-type definitions, which postulate certain properties open to discovery by ordinary methods of observation. But, as Hume noted, the fact that something has a certain property – even, in an extreme case, the property of being commanded by a god – is never, by itself, a reason for acting in one way rather than another. Something else, not my powers of observation, but (to anticipate) something connected with my wants, wishes, or aspirations – the motiva-

tional side of my being – has to be embodied in the theory. And this the naturalist fails to do. Does the non-naturalist do any better? Clearly not. We can ask, just as we could with the naturalist theories, why the fact that I have detected some non-empirical feature of an action should make any difference to my doing or not doing it. Merely postulating an extra-sensory mode of detection is no answer. One would have to postulate yet another mysterious feature: a psychological mechanism connecting the supposed property with the motivational side of human nature.

I should now like to draw together some of these objections under three headings which will enable us to formulate three tests which any satisfactory moral theory must pass. (Very few do.) I shall revert to them from time to time as we review other theories still to come.

(1) This is our initial difficulty (objection 1). Non-naturalism is metaphysically embarrassing, because it involves peculiar properties, not accessible to ordinary methods of observation or reasoning, and accessible only to a peculiar kind of faculty, which is itself totally inaccessible to ordinary psychological investigation. Moves of this kind are all too often declarations of ignorance dressed up as pseudo-discoveries. (Compare Addison's remark: 'Our superiors are guided by intuition, our inferiors by instinct.') This leads to the first test of a moral theory: *Does it involve occult properties?* The rejection of theories which fail this test is a mark of Empiricism, according to which nothing is to be admitted into the realm of serious discourse which is inaccessible to the methods of the sciences and their common-sense counterparts.

(2) This refers to the new point I introduced as Objection 6, about action-guiding force. Non-naturalism and naturalism both fail the test, which we can formulate thus, for any moral theory: *Does it account for the action-guiding feature of morality?* The rejection of theories which fail this test is a characteristic of what I propose to call Prescriptivism.

(3) This summarises Objections 1, 2, 3 and 4, particularly 4. Non-naturalism offers a very unconvincing account of moral controversy. Naturalism has a superficially plausible account: if two people are arguing about whether a certain state of affairs is

good or bad, it is just possible that one of them has detected certain empirically available features of the situation, while the other has made a mistake because of faulty observation or reasoning. But in the case of a dispute between two intuitionists – or, rather, between two moralists as interpreted according to the intuitionist – all he can say is that one person has (perhaps) intuited successfully – has *had* an intuition – while the other has not. But, whereas there are ways of deciding about mistakes of observation or reasoning, what possible way is there of deciding between conflicting intuition-claims, so as to say that one is genuine and the other not? This leads to a third test for moral theory: *Does it give an adequate account of the phenomena of moral controversy?* The rejection of theories which fail this test is a mark of Objectivism. (But notice that I have *not* included among my tests a requirement that moral judgments must be capable of being true or false. I regard this as still an open question. But truth is not the only form of objectivity.)

Non-naturalism having failed on all three counts, we turn next to emotivism.

CHAPTER IV

Emotivism

Emotivism emerges, historically, from the ruins of naturalism and non-naturalism in the following way. Quite simply, if moral concepts cannot be identified with either empirical concepts or non-empirical concepts, then they cannot be concepts at all, but only pseudo-concepts; they do not really have any meaning, except perhaps in some inferior sense of meaning in which exclamations and swear-words do. This is the view of A.J. Ayer in the best known version of Emotivism.[13] Ethical words, according to Ayer, serve merely to express (or evince) emotion on the part of the speaker, and to stimulate similar emotions in the hearer and perhaps prompt him to action or inaction accordingly. They are, broadly, part of the psychological mechanism of interaction between people, but they are emphatically not statements about what is or is not the case. It is very important to notice that they are not even statements about such feelings or emotions or other psychological facts. When I say that stealing is wrong (to take Ayer's example) I do not *state* that I have some sort of feeling against stealing, I just express this feeling, just as I would if I were to frown, or utter the word 'stealing' in a disapproving tone of voice, or write it with a cluster of exclamation marks, as Ayer suggests: 'You did wrong to steal that money' could equally well be expressed by 'Stealing money!!!' (As it happens, Ayer gets some – probably unexpected – support from Anthony Trollope:

'Stealing money!' occurs in just such a context (though with only one exclamation mark) in *The Last Chronicles of Barset*.[14]

Now this distinction between utterances which are proper statements, and utterances which may look like statements but are really only expressions of emotion, or something of that kind, is not new. The technical term for it – scientific, or cognitive, as opposed to emotive – was introduced by I.A. Richards,[15] but the distinction itself is older still. De Quincey in the nineteenth century distinguished between the literature of knowledge and the literature of power; and the same distinction was made by the ancient Greeks between *historia* (meaning science and history) and *rhetoric*. Of course the distinction is often perfectly obvious, with quite different forms of grammar for the two functions. We typically use indicative forms for expressing knowledge ('Copper is a conductor', 'William invaded in 1066'), and for rhetoric we may use imperatives ('Kill the tyrant', 'God save the King', 'Death before dishonour'). But grammatical form is not a sure guide to what is happening; in particular, an indicative form does not always mean that some fact is being asserted ('The weather is beastly', 'The music was fabulous').

Now in ethics, as we noted before, we use both indicatives and imperatives and other forms. Ayer insists that *whenever* we use an indicative form (X is right/wrong, Y is good/bad) we *never* actually state a fact. The form is always misleading. To say that stealing is wrong is not to say anything about stealing, any more than saying that the weather is beastly is (really) describing the weather. In both cases I am just reacting emotionally, expressing my feelings, and perhaps inviting my hearer to have similar feelings.

Earlier I linked determinism with emotivism by saying that, according to determinism, moral concepts have meaning but not application, while according to emotivism the reverse is true. We can now see why. Moral concepts, or rather terms which seem to express concepts, do have proper occasions for use, but they have no meaning, strictly speaking; they are not really concepts, they cannot figure in statements which can be true or false. Emotivism is the most extreme of the so-called non-cognitive ethical theories, those which make this last point, that moral talk contains nothing that can be true or false, nothing that can be known, or believed, but only felt. As I have said, the distinction itself is an old one, but its application to ethics is comparatively recent. There is a trace of it, as I said, in the view on justice attributed by Plato to Thrasymachus, where he says things like 'The rulers call anyone who breaks the law a "wrongdoer" and punish him accordingly', and 'When people denounce injustice, it is because they are afraid of suffering wrong': if Thrasymachus had maintained that the word 'wrongdoer' is used *only* to express the ruler's resentment and intent to punish, and that the word 'injustice' is used only to express the victim's dislike of what he calls unjust treatment, then he would have been an emotivist. Emotivism is sometimes attributed to George Santayana in 1912, but the most familiar statement is in A.J. Ayer's *Language Truth and Logic* (1936). A more elaborate but less purely emotivist version was published by C.L. Stevenson in 1947 under the title *Ethics and Language*.

Let us now see how this emotive theory fares with the three tests.

(1) Can it pass the 'no occult entities' test? Since this is the test it was specially designed to pass, because of its ultra-empiricist origins, it is not surprising that it passes this one. Certainly there are no occult properties of any kind in it.

(2) Can it pass the 'action-guiding' test? To some extent it passes this one, too, and that is why it is an improvement on both naturalism and non-naturalism. It does acknowledge the central importance of the motivational aspect of moral language. Although it lays stress mainly on expressing the emotions of the speaker, it does also mention the effect of moral language on the hearer; Ayer does speak of moral utterances stimulating emotion and action, and even of moral utterances 'having the force of commands'. This certainly seems to explain the strong effect that certain emotions, such as horror or admiration, can have on our conduct – effects which can be either inhibiting or stimulating. So emotivism does have the merit of accounting for something that genuinely is a feature of morality and an important one. Anyone who sincerely describes some action as wicked must feel strongly about it; if he didn't we should have to conclude that he was not sincere, he wasn't saying what he should be saying. Yet emotiv-

ism could still be wrong in making emotion the primary fact and action-guiding a secondary one.

(3) Does it pass the test for moral disputes? It seems at first that it will. We saw that naturalism can give only a barely plausible account of what goes on in a moral dispute, and non-naturalism or intuitionism only a wildly implausible one. Can emotivism do any better? Surprisingly, perhaps, it turns out that the occurrence of moral disputes constitutes an even worse difficulty for this purely subjectivist theory than it did for those supposedly objectivist ones. This is because the effect of emotivism is to reduce all moral issues to matters of inclination or taste; and matters of inclination or taste are, notoriously, not matters for argument; so there can be no moral issues, and no such thing as a moral dispute. But when A says that war is sometimes justified, and B says that war is always wrong, it seems too wildly paradoxical to say that there is really no dispute between them because each is merely giving vent to his feelings about war, and perhaps working on the other man to bring about a change in his feelings. Surely, we want to insist, contrary moral judgments like these, 'War is sometimes right' and 'War is never right' are genuinely incompatible, even if they may not be true and false (or false and true). There must, at least, be something in between truth or falsity, on the one hand, and the venting of emotion, on the other, which allows moral disputes to have a genuine matter at issue.

How does Ayer deal with this obvious objection? Let us look first a little more closely at what is involved in a genuine dispute, about any subject. It seems to be a matter of pure logic that, whenever any dispute occurs, if it is a genuine disagreement, one of the propositions must be false and the other true. If we were to apply this directly to moral disputes, we should have to conclude that in any genuine dispute, one of the disputed propositions, that is, one of the moral judgments, must be *true*. Ayer cannot possibly accept this, because the very reason for adopting emotivism in the first place was the (empiricist) difficulty about the verification of moral judgments. Ayer's solution to the problem of moral disputes is to make a distinction between two elements which are often confused in ordinary moral disputes: two

[52]

different *kinds* of disagreement. First, there is a disagreement *about* the (ordinary, non-moral) facts of the case, such as, what actually was done (it was his own money), or what the consequences of an action were or will be (if I tell this lie, she will die in peace); and secondly, there is disagreement *in* values, disagreement as to whether the facts are as they should be (one should not tell a lie even to a dying mother) which is not disagreement *about* anything. All genuine moral argument, according to Ayer, is of the first kind; disagreement in values is not a disagreement about anything, it is just a matter of the parties to the dispute expressing different, conflicting, feelings or attitudes; and once they recognise this, they will see that they are not really arguing at all, just as when we say that there is no disputing about matters of taste.

Now if we think about what actual moral arguments are like, I think this view will seem very contrived and unplausible. To see how it is to be criticised, we need to look at the central feature of emotivism, the idea of moral language as expressing feelings. First of all I want to brush aside an objection which is very commonly made, but is in fact entirely misplaced. This is the objection that many expressions of emotion, many emotional utterances, are not moral at all. This is undoubtedly true. 'What a marvellous day!', 'This is our last good-bye' are (probably) emotional but not moral. But as an argument this is just a logical blunder. Ayer is saying that all moral utterances are emotional utterances, but certainly not the converse. (Anyone who thinks there is an argument here might as well hold it an objection to a cognitivist theory that many statements of fact are not moral.)

Although the objection is entirely worthless as it stands, there is a hidden objection which does have a point. If all moral utterances are emotional utterances, as the theory holds, but not all emotional utterances are moral utterances, which is true, then we need an explanation of what makes some emotional utterances moral and some not; and it looks as if this explanation cannot be itself in terms of emotions, since we will need a distinction between *kinds* of emotion. But the emotivist theory has nothing to say about what distinguishes moral emotions from non-moral ones. And this strongly suggests that emotion is *not* the primary feature of morality, but only (as presumably most of us believe) a secondary one. Whatever distinguishes the moral from the non-moral (and this, we have seen, is the central question of meta-ethics) will of course distinguish moral emotions from non-moral ones, just as it will distinguish moral judgments or decisions from non-moral ones. But we still don't know what this distinguishing criterion is; and emotivism doesn't tell us.

However, the main objection to emotivism, and a quite fatal one, is just the fact that it does assign a central place to matters of feeling, taste, or inclination. The difference between these and whatever we express in moral judgments is all-important and cannot be theorised away. It can be summed up in the word 'Reason'. Emotivism certainly accounts for (part of) the action-guiding feature of morality: it goes some way to explaining how morality makes a difference to conduct. But it entirely omits the element of reason. Actions are guided by feelings, not reason; and this comes pretty near to saying that they are not guided at all.

How does the element of reason enter into conduct, in a way in which the emotivist elements do not? What is the difference between saying that something is right or wrong, and expressing a liking or dislike of it? There are two important differences, each of which can be regarded as a very basic function of reason: namely, consistency.

First: if I do something because I ought to do it, I shall have to be ready to say that, if ever the circumstances were to recur, I ought to do the same thing on that other occasion too. I am, we may say, committed to it, to a *policy* of action. However I make up my mind what it actually is that I ought to do here and now, I am committed to saying that I ought to do it not just here and now but wherever and whenever the occasion occurs, if it ever does; and I ought to have done it in the past if any similar occasion did occur. Now all this is not true of feelings. If I do something, not because I ought to do it, but because I feel like doing it, there is no reference to future or past occasions in this way, no commitment to consistency or a policy of action. I can't tell what I shall feel like on future occasions, and even if I could it will make no difference to what I am to do now; nor does it make any difference what I

[54]

may have felt in the past. This difference between the moral situation and the feeling situation, this consistency feature, is often summed up in the term Universality, or Universalisability. What I ought to do now, or what I hold to be right or wrong now, is what I ought always to do, or to think right or wrong. Moral judgments refer beyond the particular case, in a way in which feelings do not. The essential universality in this temporal dimension – they apply to actions of mine whether present, future or past – is at least part of the difference between moral judgments and emotions. It is also part of what is meant by speaking of moral *principles*. And this too is a function of reason. Only a rational being can have principles, though non-rational beings can have feelings and even express them. Here, then, is one aspect of moral universality.

But there is a second dimension in which morality requires consistency and universality. If I do something because I ought to do it, and not just because I feel like doing it, I must be ready to say, not merely that *I* ought to do it whenever circumstances of the same kind recur, but that anyone else ought to do it, if he is in those circumstances. This is a point I made in criticising intuitionism, that it is a necessary feature of morality that we judge others. In other words, moral judgments are universal in a second way: they apply to everyone, not just to me. But it would be even more absurd, in the case of emotions, to say that if I feel emotionally moved towards or away from something, then everyone else must do so too; just as absurd as it would be to say that what other people feel or feel like need make any difference to what I feel like doing. This second kind of universality removes me still further from the centre of things. Not only do my judgments about good and evil have to apply to others; the reverse is true as well, and it can actually be difficult to get ourselves to see that the judgments we make about others have to apply to us as well. Hence the need for the maxim to practise what you preach; and I suspect that the force of the biblical maxim 'Judge not, that ye be not judged' is 'Be careful about judging other people, because what you say about them you must, in consistency, say about yourself, and that might be awkward'. Again, the contrast with feelings is stark. I *can* have feelings about what other people do; but it would be absurd to suppose that, because I enjoy the cavortings of a ballerina, I must, should or do enjoy doing that kind of thing myself.

Moral judgments and decisions, then, are universal in this second way as well, and this again brings in the idea of principles, and the function of reason in the shape of consistency. When we judge an action, it makes no difference whose action it is. Emotivism resembles intuitionism in neglecting this feature and going instead for an excessive egocentricity.

Ayer is not, to be sure, entirely consistent in his emotivism. He speaks at one point of a 'system of values'; and the word 'system' hints at the rational element. But to admit this is to abandon a clear-cut emotivist theory, for emotions as such do not form systems. But could the features of reason that I have mentioned be incorporated in a more sophisticated emotive theory? It might be possible, for instance, to introduce feelings which are not directed to particular situations but are somehow 'about' whole classes of actions; or special kinds of desire or want, which are not directed to things that I want for myself, but to things I want for everyone, or that I want everyone to want. The word 'attitude' has been much used in such developments. But I think these attempts to salvage emotivism are not worth the effort, not at least before we have explored other possibilities.

CHAPTER V

Prescriptivism (1): The legal model

In discussing emotivism, we saw (p.52) that contrary moral judgments, like 'Wars are sometimes right' and 'War is always wrong' must be genuine contraries; there must be a real opposition between them; and if the judgments are not or false (so that the opposition between them would be that between true and false statements) then there must be something sufficiently like truth and falsity to satisfy the objectivity test; there must be something other than merely resorting to emotion. We also saw, at the end of the last chapter, that morality requires an element of consistency or universality, which can also be expressed in terms of principles. And it is very clear, thirdly, that a principle is action-guiding: having principles makes a difference to how we behave.

Now principles are rules of action; and the simplest kind of rule of action (not counting rules of games, which are only about make-believe actions) is a law. By looking at the idea of a law, we may get a *model* for moral discourse which is better than anything we have had so far. Of course moral principles are not the same as laws, but if they are sufficiently similar, and if we can explain the differences, we shall have a satisfactory ethical theory. Any such theory I am going to call by the name Prescriptivism, though this label is standardly applied rather more narrowly to the work of Professor Hare.

Before looking at the relevant features of laws and legal statements, I must enter a warning that my remarks are merely schematic, intended only to show up, by contrast, certain features of morality. A proper account of the nature of law is itself another large philosophical subject – that of jurisprudence: a meta-legal enquiry comparable to the present meta-ethical enquiry. To avoid having to carry on both enquiries at once, I must simply assume agreement on at least some broad general features of law, and I shall put in occasional token reminders that these are only approximations.

First, a feature which connects directly with the topic of the last chapter, on disputes and contradictions. An important distinction is made in law between disputes as to matters of fact and disputes as to matters of law; and this has an obvious bearing on Ayer's distinction between disagreements of fact and disagreement in value. In law, the distinction is institutionalised in the law courts, where entirely different officials or official bodies are appointed to decide the different kinds of dispute: the jury and the judge. The first kind of dispute concerns matters of fact. In the legal case, given certain laws, and given that an offence has allegedly been committed, the jury has to decide whether it has in fact been committed. The other kind of dispute is a matter of law: given that certain things have been done, the judge has to know whether or not there is a law prohibiting that kind of thing. (After all, the police might have made a mistake.) Now it is interesting to note that the question whether or not there is a certain law, is itself in its own way a matter of fact. Indeed that is why judges and counsel have the courtesy title of 'learned': it is their job to know things of this kind.

If we move over to the moral cases, it is obvious that the first kind of dispute is in place here too – we can't condemn someone morally until we know what he did. But it is very far from obvious that the second kind of dispute is in place. As we have seen, Ayer explicitly denies this: at this stage there are only different people expressing different feelings. Most of us, however, to tend to assume that some kind of moral reference-points are somehow 'there', independently of any of the parties appealing to them, though we are hard put to it to explain just what we mean by 'there'.

Let us now tabulate some similarities, and then some difference, between legal and moral rules.

(1) As we have just seen, both can be *appealed to*; that is, they can be a source both of *judgments about* actions, whether about actions already done, in the form of critical comment, or about possible actions, in the form of advice; and also of *prescriptions of* actions to be done, or avoided. The structure of this is as follows:

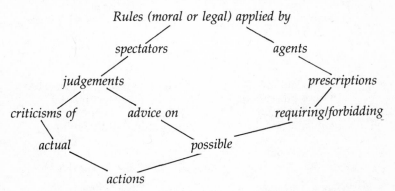

(2) Both legal and moral rules, when applied, lead to the same set of predicates conforming to a certain logical pattern (called deontic logic). We have a fourfold classification depending on the two distinctions between an act and its omission, and between prescribing and not prescribing (see Table 1 on p.60).

Notice that Class (A) and Class (D) are exact contradictories; so are Classes (B) and (C); while (A) and (B) are contraries. It is clear that opposition is well catered for here.

(3) Both legal and moral rules apply to an indefinitely large number of people, not just to an individual or a select group. (This is only approximately true, of course. Legality is considerably restricted by national frontiers; even morality may be restricted, as in the case of a tribe. But even tribal morality must contain *some* provision for dealing with aliens.)

(4) All legal rules, and all the rules of ordinary morality (the qualification is needed to exclude certain religious moralities of an unusually exacting kind) require *simple* acts of conformity. What is required by these rules is, and must be, within the normal powers of everyone to whom they apply. I am required by the

Table 1:

(A) P (X) (X is prescribed)
  X is required
  compulsory
  legally
    obligatory
  morally
    obligatory
  a duty
  one must do X
  one ought to do X

(B) P (–X) (not doing X is
    prescribed)
  X is prohibited
  forbidden
  illegal
  a crime
  a legal offence
  a sin
  a moral offence
  wrong
  one must not do X
  one ought not do X

(C) –P (–X) (not doing X is
    not prescribed)
  X is permitted
  not illegal
  not wrong
  (all) right
  one may do X

(D) –P (X) (X is not prescribed)
  X is optional
  not compulsory
  discretionary
  not a duty
  one need not do X
  all right not to do X

law, among many other things, not to assassinate Mrs Thatcher; and this is fairly easy for me not to do. There could not be a law requiring everyone to enumerate the number of miles walked each year. I am required by conventional morality not to tell lies; this again is usually easy to comply with. It cannot be a moral requirement (except in some fanatical sect) to avoid causing harm to even the minutest form of living creature. On the other hand, if there is to be any *point* in requiring or prohibiting things, there must be things which, while normally easy for me to do or avoid, might on certain occasions, such as occasions of temptation, be not so easy to do or to avoid; but even then they must still be within my power. If I am literally incapable by virtue of paralysis or irresistible compulsion, then I am not one of those to whom the rule applies.

Before going on to the differences between law and morality, which of course are going to raise difficulties, let us see how the legal theory copes with the three tests.

(1) This seems an obvious pass: there don't seem to by any occult properties in the legal field. However, we may suspect they will appear when we move on to the differences.

(2) This is an obvious pass, since the whole purpose of the legal system is to control people's conduct.

(3) This is an obvious pass, as appears from our discussion of legal disputes.

Now for the differences. It turns out that in nearly every case the law has some feature which can be readily identified and located in our day to day experience, but which morality appears to lack. Consequently there is a tendency to seek out a corresponding feature for morality, which however can no longer be assigned to our ordinary, worldly existence but seems to call for a transcendental, non-empirical status for morality, so going against requirement (1). For example, one feature of laws (to anticipate) is that they are always limited in time and place; this suggests, by contrast, that morality is unlimited in time and place, and is therefore ubiquitous and eternal.

Here is a table, with notes to follow, of the relevant aspects of law. If there were a parallel column for morality, it would be either blank, or studded with question marks.

   (i)   Author, legislator
  (ii)   Codified
 (iii)   Consensus
 (iv)   Sanctions
  (v)   Limited in (a) time (change)
                    (b) place (variety)
 (vi)   Subject to (moral) criticism
(vii)   (a) Negative
         (b) External
         (c) Regulative

(i) Every law has its author, who is called the legislator, or legislative body. (Of course not all laws originate in this way, but this is the standard way.) What he, or the institution, does can be expressed as 'I (we) hereby declare that X be henceforth illegal' or 'illegal from January 1st, 1986'. But it would be absurd for someone to get up and say 'I hereby declare that adultery (or whatever) be immoral as from January 1st'. Not only would this be a mark of insanity (it would, after all, be equally insane for any private citizen to get up and make the 'legal' statement), but we cannot imagine any possible institutional framework which could vest an individual or body with the power to utter such a (moral) pronouncement. There is, indeed, a moral analogy for the lawyer, as opposed to legislator. Both legal adviser and moral adviser can advise that something *is* wrong; but no moralist can *make* something wrong in the way the legislator can. There is, obviously, a possible exception here in God, the divine legislator. We will deal with this possibility later.

(ii) Laws are codified, morality is not. Again, neither of these is wholly true, but true enough to constitute an important difference. It isn't quite true that morality is not codified: we do in fact speak of a moral code, or a system of values. But this is obviously only a very rough approximation, compared to a legal code or system. There are some exceptions to the law being codified. There is the so-called unwritten law, such as the common law of England (as opposed to statute law). There is also case law, where the law comes into being, as it were, as a result of a series of decisions by judges in particular court actions (leading cases). But this is hardly an exception, as it amounts to a progressive, as opposed to a once and for all, codification. The importance of this codification feature is that there is (virtually) always a *decision procedure* for legal cases: a definite, public set of criteria, known by professional experts and knowable by anyone, for deciding whether some act is right or wrong. This is notoriously not the case in morals. When we come to item (vi), we shall see why morality cannot be codified.

(iii) Another important, and connected, feature distinguishing law from morality is that laws cannot conflict. Again there are rare exceptions; but it must be regarded as a serious defect of any legal system if any two legal measures lead to conflicting verdicts in a particular case. But moral principles and moral obligations frequently do conflict, and this cannot be regarded as an institutional defect, but rather as something in the very nature of morality. Consider, for instance, the conflicts between justice and mercy (as classically portrayed in *The Merchant of Venice*), or the fact that one person's freedom inevitably diminishes another's. In other words, there is characteristically, and necessarily, a virtual consensus about what the law requires, whereas there is frequently and characteristically dissensus or disagreement about what morality requires. A society without an agreed law – one in which widely discrepant legal systems were operating – could not function as a society; it will have disintegrated into splinter groups. (Something like this is said to have been the origin of the American Civil War, with disagreement about such things as the legal obligation to return fugitive slaves.) Widely divergent moralities, however, can and do coexist within a society; though it is true that if the divergencies are extreme, they will lead to political action and fragmentation; however this is a fact about politics rather than morals.

Again, there cannot be unsettled questions about what the law is, though it certainly can be an unsettled question whether the law is what it ought to be. With morals the situation is quite different. It is very frequently an open question what morality requires, and it is quite possible for a serious and rational person to disagree with another, or even with the majority. Perhaps it is conceivable that if people were serious and rational *enough*, they would all agree about what morality requires; but the fact is they never have. Notice also that the distinction between what the law is, and what is ought to be, does not apply to morals. We cannot distinguish between what morality requires, and what it ought to require. At least, we can do this only by using the term 'morality' to refer to a *particular* morality: a particular set of moral beliefs held by a particular person or group of people at a particular time. It is in this sense that we can speak of the morality of Edward Heath, or of the middle-class housewives of Aberdeen, or of the Ulster Protestants. But of course none of these is what is meant by morality as such. We can say that the morality of one of these persons or groups requires certain things that it ought not to require, just as we can say this about particular laws. But we cannot say this about morality as such, morality unqualified. Of course it may be questioned whether there is such a thing as morality unqualified. I shall come back to this when I come to points (v) and (vi).

(iv) Law has its sanctions, but it is very questionable whether morality has sanctions and, if it does, what they are. Mill devotes a whole chapter of *Utilitarianism* to this question. Let us remind ourselves of the three main functions of courts of law. We have already seen two of them: there are questions of *fact* to be decided, and this is the function of the jury. Then there are questions of *law*, and this is the function of the judge. But there is a third question: the question of penalty, or sentencing. This happens to be a second, but quite separate, function of the judge; but there may well be legal systems in which a third functionary performs the office of sentencing. Now is there such a thing as a moral sentence? Can a moral offender be subjected to moral punishment? What could such a moral sanction be? Obviously there is no formal procedure of sentencing. But perhaps we can find an analogy in things like social disapproval, ostracism, moral censure, withdrawal of friendship – these look like external sanctions – and perhaps there are internal ones, such as the unpleasant feeling we call remorse or a guilty conscience. Certainly all these are things we suffer from and wish to avoid, and perhaps our dislike of them operates like the threat of punishment in legal contexts. But there is something rather odd here. We seem to have a case of rules being broken with no consequences except that people, or the person himself, just recognise that they *have* been broken. Certainly there are rules like this: the rules of games, for instance. If I start pushing my chess pieces about anyhow, I shall not incur a penalty, other than the recognition that I am not playing chess. But morality is surely not like that. There is some sort of powerful pressure behind social disapproval, or an uneasy conscience, which needs explaining.

(v) Laws are restricted to times and places, as morality is not. Laws both change over time, and vary between regions. Now, as I noted in advance, if we apply the opposite terms to morality, we shall find ourselves saying that morality is immune to change and variety, and this seems tantamount to saying that it is eternal and ubiquitous, absolute in time and space; but this seems far too controversial to be derived from a simple contrast with law. So there is a problem here.

Let us take an actual case. Slavery became illegal in the USA with the passing of the Thirteenth Amendment in 1865; but it would be absurd to say that it became immoral then, or at any other time. If it *was* immoral in 1865, then that no doubt was *why* it was made illegal, but if it was *immoral* then, it was also immoral at any other time. Similarly the sale of alcohol was illegal during the Prohibition years (1920 to 1933) but the immorality, if such it was, did not begin and end then. As for place: slavery was already illegal in British territories in 1833, so in 1840, say, it was illegal in one place, such as Jamaica, but not in another, such as Carolina. But again it would be absurd to say that it was immoral in one place but not in another. At first sight you might think this could be defended. Suppose the slave-masters in the second place were decent, kindly, humanitarian people who treated their slaves well, while in the first place the masters were brutal slave-drivers; might you not want to say that slavery was immoral in the first place but not in the second? Well, you might want to say that and in one sense you could be right, but not in the sense that slavery is right in one place and wrong in another. It only looks like that because of a sophistry. There is a crucial ambiguity. *Either* we think that slavery is unconditionally bad – bad, irrespectively of how kind or unkind the masters may be – in which case *it* is wrong in both places, even the place where the masters are kindly; *or* we think that slavery is all right whenever the masters are decent and kind, in which case *this* too will be right in both places. Even where the masters are unkind, we can still say that slavery with kind masters is right.

So, moral principles apply to all times and places and are not subject to change and variety. Yet this may look odd. Surely it is a fact that moral principles *are* subject to change and variety. Certainly they come to be adopted, replaced, or abandoned during certain periods, in certain areas, by certain persons or groups of people. To take a simple case: surely it does make sense to say that a tribe which always had a certain moral practice actually changed it, and at a quite specific time: just after certain missionaries had visited the tribe. (I once read a newspaper report about Roman Catholic missionaries in a remote region of Vietnam. They found it hard going with a certain tribe. The tribesmen had practised the ritual killing of bullocks in sacrifice to

[65]

their gods. But they could not be made to understand that it was wrong to kill bullocks in this way, but right to drink the blood of a man called Jesus who died a long time ago. But this exception proves the rule. Missionaries have very often succeeded.) Suppose the example is cannibalism. Should we say that a certain moral principle, about eating people, had changed? Of course not; all that happened was that the tribesmen abandoned one principle and embraced another. From the point of view of everyone concerned, what happened was that a practice came to be *thought* wrong which actually *was* wrong. The tribesmen will be sorry about what they used to do, and the missionaries will be glad that the tribesmen have ceased their former evil ways. (I hope I need not say that this caricature of missionary work implies no judgment about the rights and wrongs either of cannibalism or of missionism.)

Regret and remorse have no place in legal contexts, just because this distinction between what *is* wrong and what is *thought* wrong does not apply. Legislating against X is not a case of coming to *think* that X is legally wrong; it is a case of X coming to *be* legally wrong. Consider the case of retroactive legislation. There are always strong objections, both legal and moral, to the idea that someone might be punished for an offence which was not an offence at the time he acted, because the law had not then been passed. But morality itself is necessarily retroactive, or rather retrospective. If something is now thought wrong, the thinking will date from a particular time and will presumably cease to be thought at some future time, but the *content* of the thinking, the wrongness, is not thus bounded; I can now think that something *was* wrong even if it happened before I thought so, or even existed.

There is also a parallel in the spatial dimension. It makes perfectly good sense, logically speaking, though not necessarily morally, to be a moral missionary, but no sense at all to be a legal missionary. A moralist can without absurdity claim that headhunting in Borneo is wrong and see it as his job to change this; but a lawyer cannot without absurdity complain that the French are all driving illegally on the wrong side of the road.

The distinction between what *is* wrong and what is *thought*

[66]

wrong is the same as the distinction I drew under item (iii), between morality unqualified and the morality of a particular person or group. We can now see this as another version of the third requirement – the Objectivity requirement – that I said (p.48) any satisfactory ethical theory must account for. It must incorporate, and not explain away, the distinction between something being wrong, and being thought wrong.

(vi) Laws are subject to criticism in a way in which morality is not. A legal decision may be legally ultimate – if it is made by the highest court of appeal – but it is still not ultimate in every sense. It can still be challenged on moral grounds. There is a higher authority in this sense. There are two points here. First, what is legally right can be morally wrong, and vice versa. This is a commonplace, and is illustrated by every example of the conscientious objector (the classical example was Sophocles's heroine Antigone; not, however, Socrates); and also his counterpart who might be called the unconscientious conformist (examples are those who commit evil acts when acting under orders). But, further, there is a sense in which the conflict can only be resolved in one way: in favour of morality; this constitutes the 'higher authority', or the ultimacy, of morals, which can also be illustrated in other ways. In legal contexts, there may be perplexities or uncertainties which judges decide in the light of moral considerations. Often they will determine the severity or leniency of a sentence from a moral point of view. New legislation may be introduced, or old laws repealed, because changing moral views need to be reflected in the law, or the enforcement of out-of-date legislation becomes morally objectionable.

It may seem, however, that it is not always true that a conflict between law and morals must always be settled in favour of morality. Obviously as a matter of brute fact an immoral sentence may be executed, as it was in the case of both Antigone and Socrates. But even to allow this is to leave the last word with morality: the sentence was *immoral*. The state's wrongful exercise of power does not diminish the authority of morals. But there is a more subtle sense in which the law can appear to win. One can decide to bow to the powers that be, even while recognising that their decision was wrong. This was the case with Socrates. One can decide to let the law prevail. This will happen if one thinks there is an independent moral obligation to obey the law, whatever it requires. Most of us agree that there is; it is what we call respect for law. Even those who profess civil disobedience usually claim to respect the law. It is also much the same as political obligation. Given this respect for law, it is only when the content of a law, or of a legal decision, is *seriously* immoral that the obligation to obey is outweighed by a greater obligation to defiance. So that even when, like Socrates in prison with a chance to escape, one decides to bow to the law, this is still itself a moral decision and morality is still superior.

We can see from this the explanation of item (iii), that morality cannot be codified into a book of rules. Whenever we have a system of rules, whether of a game, a club, or of law, we appeal to the rules when we wish to criticise acts which violate them; but we can't criticise the rules themselves, not even one of them, except by going outside the system; and whatever we appeal to outside the system we must regard as superior to, more authoritative than, the system. Cock-fighting no doubt has its rules, which can be invoked to criticise participants in this sport when they break a rule. But when we say that the whole game is illegal, we make *this* criticism by appealing to something outside the system. Here we are thinking of the law as superior. And the law in turn can be criticised, as we have seen, by appealing to morality. But if the rules of morality were to be codified into a system, then we should again have a set of rules which could be looked at from the outside, and criticised. But we cannot do this, for morality is ultimate, and so morality cannot be a system.

There are two apparent exceptions to this. First, there is the distinction I have already referred to twice, between morally unqualified, and morality as adopted or practised by a particular person or group – the distinction between what *is* wrong and what is *thought* wrong. Now the second sort of morality certainly can be criticised. Let us now introduce a pair of terms to mark this distinction more clearly. Morality as actually practised by particular people, we call *positive* morality (the term has nothing to do with negative, but with positivist theories about morals, law and values); morality as such, or morality unqualified, we will call *autonomous* morality. Then we can say that positive morality can be criticised exactly as laws can: from the point of view of autonomous morality; but autonomous morality cannot itself be criticised. All criticism requires a point of view from which if cannot itself be criticised.

The second apparent exception is more difficult to recognise, because it requires us to accept that *our own* morality is open to criticism. Of course there is a weak and uninteresting sense in which my morality is open to criticism: the sense in which I have to expect that other people may in fact criticise it. If my considered moral judgment is criticised, I shall not allow that the critic is right; I shall claim that he is mistaken. For I cannot allow that my judgment is wrong, or even that it is just as likely to be wrong as right. There is no difference here between moral and factual beliefs: if I believe something, I cannot also believe that my belief is false, or even that it is as likely to be false as true.

But there *is* a sense in which I *can* be self-critical. I can adopt a critical attitude to my own moral judgments and decisions; but I can only do this by *detaching* myself from them in a special way – by *not* treating them as fully considered judgments. It is possible to detach oneself in this way. I can come to regard my own morality – or at least part of it, for part of the time – in the same way as I regard someone else's morality – as another case of positive morality (in the sense defined above). This is perhaps most likely to happen if I have been brought up in a particularly strict (or even a particularly lax) way, and I find myself reacting to situations which call for moral judgment, in ways which on second thoughts I don't really approve of. When I really think about the matter – when I consider my unconsidered judgments – I don't think I should feel so guilty about X, or else I think I really ought to have more scruples about doing Y. This sort of conflict between the product of moral training (or the lack of it) and the product of mature moral thinking, calls for a pair of terms. Perhaps we might call them the Freudian and the Reflective Conscience. My reflective conscience, the voice of reason, can disapprove of (or, of course, back up) my Freudian conscience, the voice of unreason. But this only means that the morality which is immune to criticism is the reflective, autonomous morality.

(vii) The last feature I want to look at which seems to contrast law and morality is that law has something essential *negative* about it in a way that morality does not. Care is needed here: if we say, by contrast, that morality is, or may be, positive, this means something entirely different from the positive morality discussed under item (vi).

(a) Here is a quotation from a book called *Ethics for Modern Business Practice*:

> There is a difference between law and ethics: law tells one what he should *not* do, whereas ethics tells one what he *should* do.

Now I shall agree that law *is* negative, but it is by no means clear that ethics isn't negative too. First, let us establish this negative characteristic of law. It is that the fundamental reason for the existence of law is as a form of control; and to control people's conduct by legal means is very largely a matter of preventing them from doing things which they would be likely to do if not so prevented, things which would be harmful to society. Law prevents these things by making them *offences*. This is well brought out by the following case: some new legislation was introduced to control motorists, and I noticed that it was announced in a newspaper headline as NEW TRAFFIC OFF-ENCES PROPOSED. This could sound bizarre; but this is because the two different sorts of negation operating here (see p.59) generate two different kinds of offensive situation: one is where an existing practice is made illegal, the other is where an existing law is infringed. Parliament proposes offences in the first sense; the drunken, unlicensed car driver proposes offences in the second sense. But in either case, the point is that law and offence go together.

But isn't morality negative in precisely the same way? When Moses came down from Mount Sinai, couldn't this event have been reported in a newspaper headline as NEW MORAL OFF-ENCES PROPOSED? After all, 'Thou shalt not kill' does not 'tell one what he *should* do'. It is sometimes said that the ethics of the Old Testament is indeed negative and inhibitive, but that the ethics of the New Testament is more positive. There is something in this; but formally, at least, 'Render unto no man evil for evil', though more enlightened and even inspiring, is purely negative. Nor is there anything very positive, it seems, about the virtue of meekness. However, part of the difficulty here is that many actions and states of mind can be described both positively and negatively: in the example, revenge is non-forgiveness, forgiveness is not taking revenge.

(b) But there is a clue here to something more substantial. There is such a thing as blind revenge, whereas there is no such thing as blind forgiveness. (It could not, for instance, be distinguished from forgetfulness.) Forgiveness implies a definite, positive state of mind, a certain intention on the part of the agent, reflecting a certain character and a virtue of tolerance rather than the vice of vindictiveness. Now states of mind, what the agent intends to do, what his motives were, what his character is, what his virtues and vices are, are all highly relevant to any *moral* judgment of what he does; but they are *not* always relevant to a legal judgment. Of course in some cases, some of them are: the difference between murder and manslaughter, for instance, is defined in terms of the intentions of the agent. *Mens rea* is an important criterion of criminal responsibility. But it is by no means always relevant, in cases of strict liability, for instance. If a baker sells a cake with a dead beetle in it, he doesn't escape liability by pleading, however truthfully, that he didn't intend there to be a beetle in it. So this helps to fill out the negative-positive contrast. The law is typically concerned only with externals; with acts to be prevented; while morality is also concerned with internals: with intentions and motives which have a bearing on character. And while certain character-traits, called vices, need to be suppressed, others, the virtues, need to be fostered and encouraged: and this is a very positive function. We should remind ourselves at this point that the very word 'ethics' originally meant the study of character-formation.

(c) Another way of filling out what is meant by the positive aspect of morality is to contrast the *regulative* function of law, and of *some* morality (such as the 'Old Testament' type) with what we might call the *aspirational* aspects of morality: our strivings for the good, as opposed to our shrinkings from evil. Morality is not, or not merely, a form of social control; it is also the expression of

[71]

personal aspirations. When we consider the morality of the saint, the hero, or the martyr, the legal analogy seems to fail. But, as we shall see, these cases raise special problems for ethics too; they do not seem to fit the picture of consistency and universal applicability. We shall consider this problem in Chapter X.

Customs

After this lengthy discussion of the similarities and differences between legal and moral rules, let us glance very briefly indeed at something more primitive than either, from which it is generally thought they have both developed: the notion of custom, usage or tradition. (The word *morals* originally means matters of custom.) Customs certainly share the features which law and morals have in common (p.59). They are obviously action-guiding: certain things are criticised as 'not done'. They apply to everyone, or at least to everyone in the largest relevant group: the society or tribe. And they require simple acts of conformity. By looking at the differences, we may see how they are more like laws in one respect, more like morals in another, which may suggest how law and ethics have diverged from a common origin.

(i) Customs do not normally have an author, though in special cases they may be attributed to a founder, usually mythical. But no one can literally inaugurate a custom. This is brought out by the stock joke about the American college which had a notice saying 'This tradition will start next Monday'.

(ii) Customs are not codified, except perhaps by the anthropologists who study them. But perhaps the Book of Deuteronomy represents an effort by the Jews to codify customs that were too complicated to remember.

(iii) Customs are obviously a matter of consensus.

(iv) Sanctions may vary from a public penalty (like the law) to censure or disapproval (like morals).

(v) Customs are definitely limited in time and place.

(vi) The distinction between what is required by custom, and what ought to be required, cannot arise at the level of custom.

(vii) Custom covers both negative features, like punishment of offenders, from which law develops, and positive features, such as educational methods, which develop into the more aspirational parts of ethics.

Points (v) and (vi) are important for the development of moral thinking. Historically, the discovery that one's social rules are not the same as those of another society, has often led reflective people to search for more universal rules; and the idea that one's own set of rules might not be the right ones, might be open to correction and criticism in the light of something beyond them, is the beginning of rational morality. If all existing standards, including one's own, are open to examination, the standards of examination cannot be the existing ones. Or so it seems, and hence the idea of something universal emerges.

Before leaving the subject of customs, we might do well to remember that customs comprise all aspects of life, or culture, and not just those aspects of life that we have been considering as legal or moral. Are we justified in so restricting morality to only certain aspects of life – especially as we have not explicitly specified *which* aspects? After all, the Greeks and Romans considered the wearing of trousers to be a mark of moral inferiority. Why do we tend to exclude such matters as dress, hairstyle, or table manners, from the scope of morality? Here, of course, we return again to the central question of meta-ethics: what distinguishes the moral from the non-moral. We shall resume discussion of this aspect of it in Chapter XI. In the meantime the subject of customs leads naturally to the problem of relativism.

CHAPTER VI

Relativism

Some forms of ethical relativism are trivially true, for instance relativity to circumstances. If there is a moral requirement to the effect 'Whenever you are in situation A, always do X', the wrongness of doing Y instead of X will *depend on*, will be *relative to*, the circumstances: on whether I am in fact in situation A or not. If asked whether it would be right or wrong to do Y, it would be perfectly proper to reply 'It depends on the circumstances'. This is true of all possible moral theories.

But suppose I get the answer: 'It depends on your moral principles'. This invokes a much more radical and controversial kind of relativism. It implies that moral principles can *vary*, just as circumstances can. And this is contrary to most people's deep convictions.

Relativism, in this second sense, is one of the major types of theory about the nature of morality. It is a reductionist theory, almost as challenging as emotivism, but rather more defensible. It is usually thought to deny the existence of what I have called autonomous morality, or morality unqualified, and to leave room only for positive morality – the actual practices and principles of a particular society at a particular time. However, this is a mistake. What relativism does deny is absolutism or realism.[16]

Relativism is a theory which takes very seriously what I have called the legal model, holding in effect that moral principles and norms do exist, but in very much the same way as laws do, with only some simple and easily explained differences. And obviously we don't need a relativist theory of laws, because it is only too obviously true.[17] According to the ethical relativists, the seven major differences we noted between law and morals, all of which tended to suggest some transcendent status for morality, can be dealt with, either by explaining or denying them, as follows:

(1) (Laws have authors.) Moral norms do not have authors, but this is because no single identifiable person originates them; they grow up and develop from obscure beginnings.
(2) (Laws are codified.) The relativist can accept my explanation of why moral norms are not codified.
(3) (Laws are subject to consensus.) The fact that morality is subject to disagreement is no problem for the relativist.
(4) (Laws have formal sanctions.) The relativist can emphasise the similarity of function between social pressures and penal sanctions.
(5) (Laws are limited to times and places, and subject to change and variety.) The relativist will either deny that moral principles do hold universally in time and place, explaining away our convictions to that effect as mere simple-mindedness; or he may allow that it is true in the following sense: *our* moral principles do indeed apply to all times and places; we may apply them even to people who do not themselves accept them. Even a relativist can condemn cannibalism: although the cannibals' claim that eating people is not wrong is relative to their principles, and his claim that it is wrong is relative to his principles, it doesn't follow that he isn't making a genuine moral judgment.
(6) (Laws are subject to criticism from a standpoint outside themselves.) Although moral principles cannot, for the relativist, be ultimate in any absolute sense, they can certainly be *ulterior*. Moral thinking is usually in advance of the law, so it is not surprising if the law is criticised and perhaps changed in the light of moral thinking, but not *vice versa*.
(7) (Laws tend to be prohibitive and concerned with externals, while morality allows room for aspirations and ideals,

and is essentially concerned with intentions.) This is no problem for the relativist.

One of the earliest examples of a relativist theory in the history of philosophy is the view briefly propounded by Thrasymachus in Plato's *Republic*. His view that justice is the interest of the stronger – taking this to mean that doing what is right means doing what you are told by those in power – means that moral judgments to the effect that some act is right or wrong are relative to the principles of conduct laid down by certain authorities. Some of these principles, those *enforced* by the rulers, will be laws, in which case the judgment will be a legal one; but other norms may be imposed less formally and these will be the moral ones.

Relativist theories can be developed for other fields of value than the ethical, in aesthetics, for instance, and even in the field of truth. In aesthetics we might have a Thrasymachus-type view to the effect that beauty is the current preference of the dominant school of art critics. In the field of truth, the case of Galileo and the Inquisition might suggest that truth is whatever the Roman Catholic Church requires us to believe. Or it might be held, as it actually was by certain members of the Vienna school, that truth is the set of beliefs of the scientific culture-circle. Even this is represented in antiquity: another of Plato's sophists, Protagoras, was celebrated for his view that 'Man is the measure of all things', including truth. Plato has no difficulty in demolishing the relativist theory of truth, but it is somewhat more difficult to demolish the relativist theory of the right and the good.

Apart from the similarities between law and morals, another important tendency towards relativism comes from the possibilities offered by the social sciences of explaining people's moral beliefs and principles in terms of their causes in certain other factors in society, or in human nature (though the latter, as we shall see, points more strongly the other way). This is a new kind of determinism, which aims at explaining in causal terms not actions, but the acquisition and retention of beliefs and principles. People may or may not be free to act according to, or contrary to, their beliefs and principles; but they are not, according to these higher-level deterministic theories, free to choose their beliefs and principles. Examples of these higher-level types of theory are:

(1) Psychological theories of value (Freud, Eysenck)
(2) Sociological theories (Pareto, Westermarck)
(3) Political theories (Thrasymachus, Hobbes)
(4) Economic theories (Marx)

Here is a specific example of a psychological causal theory of moral values, and its connection with relativism. The example occurred in the course of some correspondence in *The Observer*, which began with a review of a book by Lord Russell, *Why I am not a Christian*. Replying to Philip Toynbee, the reviewer, Russell wrote:

> I find my own views on ethics (that there are no absolute values) . . . argumentatively irrefutable, yet nevertheless incredible . . . I cannot meet the arguments against absolute ethical values, and yet I cannot believe that a dislike of wanton cruelty is merely a matter of taste, like a dislike of oysters . . . I do not know the solution.

Notice that Russell is referring to emotivism, which is an extreme and particularly implausible form of relativism; but what he says would apply to any other form, because relativism is first and foremost a matter of *denying* something: the existence of what Russell calls 'absolute ethical values'. This denial Russell says he finds theoretically irrefutable, yet unbelievable. In other words, it is a typical philosophical paradox: a case of a theory leading to a conclusion which is outrageously at odds with common sense. However, another writer thinks he has the answer to Russell's problem, and a solution to the paradox. He is Professor Eysenck, the psychologist, who wrote:

> The problem . . . is a purely psychological one, the answer to which is well known on the basis of extensive experimental studies.

> Why does Russell feel the way he does about wanton cruelty, to the extent of almost regarding this feeling as a reflection of 'absolute value'? Following on some Russian work, it has been shown conclusively that aesthetic, social and political beliefs and values can be conditioned in precisely the same manner as salivation was conditioned in Pavlov's

dogs, and according to the same rules of contiguity and reinforcement. The subject of such experiments acquire new values without knowing how they came to do so . . .

There is no difficulty in accounting for Russell's strong convictions in terms of a particularly strong and extended process of conditioning, coupled with a nervous system particularly liable to form stable conditioned responses. As I have pointed out in my book *The Psychology of Politics*, tender-minded people like Russell are particularly liable to possess such a type of nervous system, and although in the absence of a detailed case-history one cannot be sure, this appears to be a likely answer to his question.

Notice that Eysenck is here claiming to answer two questions at once: one about the strength of Russell's feelings about wanton cruelty (and Russell, as a matter of fact, does not mention feelings at all), and the other about Russell's belief that these feelings reflect some absolute ethical values. Now these are different questions and will not necessarily have the same answer. There is no necessary connection, in general, between strength of feeling and firmness of conviction about something 'absolute' behind the feeling. Here are two counter-examples: I have no strong feelings about the shape of the earth, yet I have a very firm conviction that the belief that the earth is round and not flat is absolutely true. On the other hand, a collector may be quite passionate about rare postage-stamps or post-Impressionist French paintings, yet he doesn't have to believe that these have anything 'absolute' about them. Even in ethics, the intensity of my feelings about cruelty to children may be less than the intensity of my agony in a purely personal predicament. It is not the *strength* of moral feelings that makes us project them towards absolute values, it is something else about them, such as the features of impersonality and universality already noted. All the same, we may agree that there is indeed a certain tendency for the serious but not deeply reflective moralist to be an absolutist; and Eysenck thinks that an explanation in terms of 'conditioning' will explain both the moral feelings and the *first* thoughts of the moral philosopher. He is saying to Russell: 'Your moral feelings are non-rational; your first thoughts in moral philosophy – absolutism – are also non-rational; and I have explained both of these in my theory. But your *second* thoughts in moral philosophy – what you find, correctly, to be theoretically irrefutable, namely anti-absolutism or relativism – these are rational, and I agree with them. Go on thinking this, and ignore the clash with what you find incredible, and you will eventually think yourself out of your conditioned responses.' (We may wonder whether Russell is here being invited to submit himself to a further course of conditioning.)

Now there is a tendency to think that if you have explained someone's values or beliefs by showing what caused them, you have somehow invalidated them, as though they no longer have the same claim to be sound, rational or correct. So a determinist theory of moral values, or a relativist theory based on it, seems somehow to undermine the values it explains; and this may make us unwilling to accept or even consider a determinist or relativist theory. So it is important to point out that the thinking here is completely mistaken. Showing that some moral belief has a cause is no more an undermining of that belief, than it would be in the case of a factual belief. If someone has a false belief, we shall often want to look for the cause of his mistake; but the cause isn't what *makes* it a mistake. If someone thinks he is Napoleon, his belief is insanely false, and we shall look for a cause in his disordered psyche. But it isn't his disordered psyche that makes it false. And if he believes something true, say that the earth is round, no doubt this belief too has a cause involving his mental processes, but the presence of a cause most certainly does not undermine the truth of his belief; if anything, it supports it. So there is no case for saying that the causal explanation of a moral belief undermines it, either.

A determinist, like Eysenck, is necessarily a relativist, but a relativist is not necessarily a determinist. To deny that there are absolute values does commit the relativist to saying what sort of thing the relativised values are instead – whether conventions, emotional attitudes, conditioned responses, elements of a positive morality, or whatever – but it does not commit him to saying why or how they are what they are, to giving a causal explanation. He can simply take these items as ultimate facts about man in the social state, not calling for any further explanation. Accordingly we shall ignore the deterministic or causal aspect of the matter from now on, and look at the argument between relativists and realists in terms of the most plausible of the types of theory listed above, which I take to be sociological relativism. This is the account of morality in terms of a set of social facts about what people do in fact approve and condemn – what I have called a positive morality.

We must look, then, at the contending theories, remembering that we cannot expect to prove or disprove either relativism or realism, but only to test each type of theory to see if it has theoretical implications which we find unacceptable. Does relativism, for instance, imply that every moral code is as good as every other, or that there is no such thing as moral progress? If so, we shall reject relativism because these consequences are plainly unacceptable. Does absolutism imply the existence of unknowables, or transcendent realities? If so, then an empirically-minded philosopher will reject it for failing the test concerned with occult entities – or Mackie's Argument from Queerness.

Absolutists have tended to speak in terms of *standards*, so I must first comment on the difference between standards and principles, since I have been tending to speak in terms of principles. Standards and principles are two different kinds of *criteria*; and a criterion is anything we use to *judge* things by (this is what it literally means). The kind of criterion called a standard enables us to make judgments in a continuous range or *scale*, using such terms as 'good', or 'poor', 'mediocre', 'excellent' and so on. The examination mark of 100 is a standard. In ethics, the virtues are standards. For example, someone might be charitable (good at giving), cowardly (poor at facing up to danger), not very industrious (mediocre at working), and so on. The thing to notice here is that all of these judgments are of the 'more or less' kind. All, that is, except judgments of perfection, which are limiting cases and typically very rare, like an examination script actually receiving a mark of 100.

When a principle or rule is used as a criterion of judgment, the judgment is not of the 'more or less' kind, but of the 'yes or no' kind, such as a verdict. Since the whole point of a principle or rule is to require or forbid the very action it describes, there is no room for anything in between doing the action and not doing it, obeying the rule and disobeying; nothing between right and wrong. In ethics, verdicts of right or wrong are quite different from assessments of good and bad.

Is either type of criterion primary? It seems that the choice of which is primary and which is secondary is characteristic of a whole style of ethical theory. If moral principles or rules are taken as fundamental, the primary moral question will be whether some act is right or wrong; and it will be a secondary question whether someone is a good or bad man, the answer to this question depending on the answer to the first: he is a good man if he does right actions, or, more correctly, if he does right actions intending to do them and intending them because they are right; and similarly for the evil man and wrong actions. Roughly, this is the position of Kant. Alternatively, if moral standards are fundamental, the primary question will be whether someone is a good or bad person, and it will be a secondary question whether some act is right or wrong: right, if it is the sort of act a good person would do, wrong, if not. Roughly, this is the position of Aristotle. Or again, if we speak fundamentally not of good and evil persons, but of good and bad states of affairs, things worth having or things to be avoided, then right and wrong will depend on whether an act brings about, or tends to bring about, a good or bad state of affairs. Roughly, this is the position of the Utilitarians.

Among moral philosophers who have been absolutists, there have been characteristic differences depending on whether they have taken standards, or principles, as fundamental. A standard which is universally applicable and independent of individuals and societies is called an absolute standard. A principle which is universally binding irrespective of who recognises or enforces it, is called a moral law. A moral law, on this view, is a principle to which we are subjected because of our very nature as human beings, or as rational agents; and these principles are to be contrasted with ordinary laws, such as the laws of the state, to which we are subjected because of something less than our full human nature, because we happen to be citizens of one particular state rather than another. They are also to be contrasted with what I have called positive morality, the ordinary working rules which we actually observe in our daily lives, to which we are subjected because of something which is again less than our full human nature, namely our fallibility and ignorance: since we are *only* human, we cannot know for sure what the moral law truly is.

Now although, as we shall see, absolutism is commonly formulated in terms of standards, it is, I think, most deeply rooted in a certain attitude to principles. If rules and principles do play a considerable part in our moral lives, we shall tend to acquire a certain attitude to them which favours absolutism in two ways, one logical and the other sociological. The logical consideration is the one I pointed out above when I distinguished principles from standards: a principle-based verdict is a matter of yes or no, not more or less, because a rule is either obeyed or disobeyed, and there are no degrees of compliance. If we do have a principle to the effect that one must not do X, then a particular case of doing X is, in an acceptable and unmysterious sense, absolutely wrong.

But, of course, this is only a logical consequence of what principles and rules are. The immediate reply should be: one cannot doubt or qualify the judgment that X is wrong so long as one accepts the rule from which indeed it 'absolutely' follows: but of course one can question the rule itself, so *this* is not absolute. Let us turn, then, to the sociological point, which is what helps to explain the grip of absolutism.

As I pointed out when I discussed the similarities and differences between morality and law, people in a society may at a certain stage of development come to be critical of their own laws, and even of their own morality – as long as we mean by 'morality' here *positive* morality, the principles and practices which they actually adopt and follow. There are important historical and cultural differences between a society in which positive morality is simply accepted without question, and a society (which may of course be the same society at a later stage of development) in which moral principles and practices are criticised in the light of new powers of reflection. Clearly the ability to question the hitherto unquestionable marks the rise of criticism and eventually philosophy, and represents a very great intellectual advance. The beginning of moral philosophy with the Sophist movement in ancient Greece is just such a stage.

Absolutism has its roots in tribal morality, as personified in the old man Cephalus in the opening scene of Plato's *Republic*. Relativism represents the dawn of self-criticism, intellectual detachment, the ability to consider one's own moral code along with those of other societies, and to ask whether it is indeed better (or worse) than they are. Absolutism as a philosophical theory, rather than a primitive and unreflective attitude, comes after relativism; as a philosophy, it must share with relativism the rejection of an uncritical attitude to customary morality, but it retains the substance of the uncritical assumptions.

What we have to deal with in the absolutist theory is a formidable combination of three elements: a deep-rooted tendency, operative in uncritical moods and tempers, to act and react as if the theory were true; a powerful philosophical tradition in its favour; and an assortment of intellectual arguments against relativism. I come now to a review of some typical arguments and counter-arguments.

Perhaps the most familiar of the arguments against relativism goes like this. We judge that one moral code is better than another; but if there is no absolute moral standard, we have no right to make such a judgment, because there is nothing in respect of which we can compare the two codes. Now this argument has two false premisses. First: if we wish to compare two things of a comparable kind, but have no standard of comparison, it is not necessarily impossible to perform the comparison. I can compare one stick with another and judge that it is the longer one, without having to use a standard length, such as a ruler. Similarly, I can perfectly well compare one moral code with another, without comparing both of them with a third. So much for the false premiss that we can compare two things only if we can compare each with a third thing. The mistake was in the 'only'. But of course we *can* compare two things by comparing each with a third thing; but then there is another false premiss. Suppose I do wish to compare the two sticks, but they cannot be brought into juxtaposition for direct comparison, and I must use some third object which can be juxtaposed with each, such as a measuring-rod. We may call this third object a standard; but there is nothing 'absolute' about it. The measuring-rod need not be, and, as we shall see shortly, cannot be, an absolute standard. Whether it is an extremely accurate or an extremely inaccurate replica of the standard metre does not make the slightest difference to its effectiveness in measuring the comparative lengths of the two sticks. All that matters is that I should adopt it as my standard for the purpose in hand, and stick with it. And similarly in the case of ethics: I can use a third code as a standard by which to judge the comparative merits of two other codes; but whether it is like or unlike the absolute standard makes no difference to the possibility of comparison. All that matters, again, is that I should adopt it; that it should be *my* code of ethics; and that I should stick with it, that is use it consistently. All that is needed for me to judge that one moral code is better than another, is that I should *have* a moral code; not that there should be an 'absolute' code as well.

We can demonstrate the structure of code-comparing by means of the following schematic exercise. It involves several simplifying assumptions, some grossly so, but such oversimplification is often necessary, at least initially, if theory is to get to grips with the complexities of real life. The assumptions are these: (1) that a moral code consists of a set of rules; (2) that every rule is prohibitive; (3) that rules can be simply identified as R_1, R_2, etc., and that different codes differ only in adding some rules or leaving out others; (4) that the terms identifying the type of action prohibited are (a) purely descriptive, and (b) mean exactly the same in different codes; (5) that all the rules are of equal weight. This last assumption needs clarifying. In real life, if there is a conflict between moral considerations for and against some course of action, we frequently resolve the conflict by deciding that one consideration is weightier than, more important than, the other. Saving a life is more important than keeping a promise. If we wished to incorporate this feature in a code, there would have to be second-order rules according to which a conflict between rules R_1 and R_2 is to be settled in favour of R_1, say, or R_2. But we are ignoring this in the present exercise.

Consider now two mini-codes C_1 and C_2, each of which consists of a selection of rules from a maximum set of five. These five possible rules are prohibitions on the following: slavery, incest, suicide, alcohol, and lying:

$$C_1 : R_1 \; R_2 \; - \; R_4 \; R_5$$

$$C_2 : \; - \; R_2 \; R_3 \; R_4$$

It follows immediately that adherents of C_1 will criticise C_2-holders for being too permissive about slavery and lying (since they do not prohibit them) and also for being too censorious about suicide (which they prohibit); while C_2 people will criticise C_1-holders for being too censorious and too permissive, respectively, about the same things. So far we have pure relativism. But clearly C_1 and C_2 can *both* be appraised. The absolutist claims that this can be done only by invoking some absolute code C_0, which contains an eternally fixed and final selection of Rs. Suppose it is:

$$C_0 : R_1 \; R_2 \; R_3 \; - \; R_5$$

Now by comparing both C_1, and C_2 with C_0 we see at once that, according to C_0, C_1 is defective in two respects (it is too permissive about suicide and too restrictive about alcohol), while $C2$ is defective in three respects. One code is therefore better than the other, which is the result we wanted. But it should be clear from my example of the sticks that this result did not require C_0 to be 'absolute', or to be anything more than a third code alongside C_1 and C_2. So the code-comparing argument is no objection to relativism.

Another favourite argument of the absolutist is that, on the relativist view, there can be no such thing as moral progress or moral decline. To this the short answer is that there can indeed be no 'absolute' progress, but there can be progress. Another argument is that on the relativist view, moral effort and striving become meaningless. This too begs the question; but I shall leave a more detailed discussion of both moral progress and moral effort for a separate section to follow.

First, let me return to the main absolutist argument about code-comparing, in order to show that it is not merely ineffective, but positively self-defeating. We have seen that, for the purpose of comparing codes, an absolute standard is not necessary. We can now go further and show that it is actually impossible. For it is an essential feature of the absolute standard that, being distinct from any humanly accessible standard, it cannot be known by human beings; for the accessible standards admittedly differ, so that either none of them is the absolute standard, or at most one of them is, but of course we do now know which. But this is fatal to the argument about comparison. For if no one ever had access to the standard metre, there would not *be* a standard metre; it could not fulfil the very function for which it is intended. Similarly, if the only condition on which people are allowed to compare two moral codes is that they should refer them to the absolute standard, they never could do so, since the condition could never be satisfied.

Absolutists wish to think, of course, that actual moral standards are approximations, in varying degrees, to the absolute standard, and that moral progress consists in increased approximations. In the light of the foregoing we must suspect that this thinking is quite vacuous, since there is no way of verifying that one thing is like or unlike another thing when there is no access to both. However, it is time to draw together the points concerned with moral progress and moral effort, and to discuss this topic in its own right. Do the facts of moral progress and decline, properly understood, support absolutism or relativism?

Moral progress

Let us ask first about the notion of progress in general, irrespective of whether we are talking about progress in morality, in transport, in literacy, or whatever. The first thing to note is that every statement about progress or regress involves two elements: (a) a statement about a *trend*; and (b) a *value-judgment*. Let us take these in order.

(a) Progress implies progression, which means literally a stepping forward. Sometimes we do mean this literally, as when we speak of the progress of a marathon runner, or almost literally, of a transatlantic yachtsman. But usually we mean some other kind of change. In either sense, progression means a continuous change in a certain direction. Something is progressing either if it gets more and more different from a certain initial state, or if it gets more and more similar to a certain final state. An example of the first kind would be the progress of motor-car design: cars have got more and more different from the horseless carriage that was their starting-point, but we cannot say that they are getting more and more like a certain final state, because we do not know what that final state would be. On the other hand, if we take the example of progress in the field of education in literacy, we do know what the final state is: it is the state in which everybody can read and write, and progress in literacy is when more and more people are able to read and write.

(b) The other element in a statement about progress is a value-judgment. If the trend, or continuous change, is rated as good, it counts as progress; if bad, as regress or decline, decadance, deterioration. It may seem too obvious to be worth stating, that we can't tell whether a change is good, bad or neither, until we look at what it *is* that is changing: some changes will be good, some bad, and some neither. But it is worth glancing at other possibilities, however bizarre they may seem. One quite influential line of thought throughout the ages has been that changes, and especially changes in human affairs, are, quite generally, by and large and on the whole, a bad thing. This idea comes in two forms. The first is that change itself is a bad thing, compared with changelessness: this idea owes much to Plato's metaphysics, and is reflected in a couple of lines of a well-known hymn:

Change and decay in all around I see;

O Thou who changest not, abide with me.

The other version is that, while change is not *necessarily* for the worse, human affairs just do *as a matter of fact* get worse and worse. The view that there is a universal tendency for human affairs to get more and more different from an initial optimum state is found in the ideas of a Golden Age, the Fall of Man, Paradise Lost.[18] It is also reflected in the fact that every generation tends to find fault with the previous generation. But this recurring complaint, however universal, is notoriously worthless.[19] And universal pessimism of this kind can be refuted by a simple, if suspect, argument. If *everything* is worse than it was, then one of the things that has got worse must be our standards of judgment; so we are more likely to be wrong in our judgments

[87]

that things *have* got worse! (One reason for glancing at the ideas of universal regress, or progress, was to enable me to introduce the idea that standards of judgment themselves are among the things that can change.)

The counterpart of universal pessimism is, of course, universal optimism: that change is just a good thing, either in itself, or as predominantly tending towards a final optimum state. This is the familiar, if now somewhat outmoded, notion of Progress. And this universal optimism, if not very plausible today, is at least immune to the corresponding argument about standards of judgment. If everything is getting better, our standards of judgment will be even better than they were, so we can be even more sure that we really are progressing! (Again, there is obviously something suspect here.)

We return now to the safer view that change is neither good nor bad in itself, but is progressive or regressive only in relation to a particular trend or trends. In order to determine whether there is or is not progress, we need to know two things: we need to know which particular changes we are talking about – whether in literacy, transport, or child mortality – and we need a standard or criterion for judging whether the change in question is good, bad, or indifferent. And it is very unlikely that we shall end up with a statement about universal progress or regress. We are only too likely to find that a trend towards X, which is a good thing, coexists with a trend towards Y, which is bad. A commonplace example is that a great increase in material comforts and consumer goods goes with a serious decline in spiritual well-being.

Now what of moral progress? According to what I have just said, we will need to consider two separate things: first, the changes we are interested in, and these are changes in morality; and second, the standards or criteria for judging those changes. And we see at once that we are going to be in trouble: because in the special case of morality (and perhaps other fields of value) these are *not* two separate things. The standards themselves are, or are very largely, the very changes we are supposed to be examining. And we have just seen the oddity of using standards of judgments to talk about changes in those very standards themselves.

[88]

Now it might be pointed out that this trouble arises only for the relativist, not for the absolutist. (If so, the facts of moral progress will indeed favour absolutism.) For, according to the absolutist, *the* standards do *not* change, even if *our* standards do. And the account of moral progress or regress will be quite straightforward. It will go like this. First, there are two sorts of changes we must consider. (At this point we introduce the notion of moral effort as well as moral progress.) One sort of change is that, as time goes on, we come to achieve a clearer grasp, understanding, awareness, of those immutable principles; or, alternatively, to lose our grip on them. But another, quite different, sort of change concerns the relation between preaching and practice. It may be that, without any change in the principles themselves, or in our grasp of them, we can nevertheless become more strict, or more lax, in our actual conformity to those principles. When people speak of the hypocrisy of the Victorian moralists, they have in mind a rather gross discrepancy between high-minded principles and a widespread covert disregard of them in practice. This second sort of change is easily dealt with. It is obvious that, given a certain set of moral principles as people understand them, a situation where those people's actual obedience to the principles they profess to believe in is stricter than it used to be, is a better situation. This follows from the truism that, if you ought to do X, then it is better if you actually do X than if you don't; or, still more truistically, if you ought to do X, then you ought to *actually* do X. So greater conformity between preaching and practice is genuinely progressive, and greater departure is regressive, involving the evils of hypocrisy, insincerity, and weakness of will. It is here that we can also locate the notion of moral effort. It *is* hard to live up to high-minded principles.

But what about the other kind of change – in our grasp or understanding of principles? Here, too, the absolutist seems to have a ready-made account of progress. First, let us set out the relevant assumptions of the absolutist view:

(1) There is a definite set of moral standards or principles, according to which certain things are definitely and truly right, or wrong, whatever people may think;

(2) These standards or principles are the same for all people;

(3) They are the same at all times.

(2) and (3) must however be qualified:

(2a) Although the principles are the same for all people, not all people fully recognise them, only some do (perhaps ourselves); or, more cautiously, no people fully recognise them, though some people (perhaps ourselves) come closer to recognising them than others do; and

(3a) Although the principles are the same at all times, they are not fully recognised at all times, but only at certain times (perhaps the present time); or, more cautiously again, at no time have they been fully recognised, though people have come closer to recognising them at certain times (perhaps at the present time) than at other times.

Now we can say what constitutes moral progress or decline. The actual morality of a community is progressive if: either: actual moralists do recognise the true moral principles whereas their predecessors did not, or: actual moralists adopt moral principles which are more like the true ones than those adopted by their predecessors. And morality will be retrogressive in the opposite cases, which I need not spell out. As examples of both moral progress and decline, we might take, first, the modern attitude to slavery as progressive; and as an example of degeneration I would cite the attitude prevalent in the West to weapons of mass destruction – the fact that 'we' are prepared to destroy entire civilian populations as an act of war, whereas our predecessors were not.

So, on the realist view of morality, moral progress and decline do make good sense. (I have, of course, for the sake of argument, been waiving the objections to the unknowability of the standards.) The field in which progress occurs is easily delineated; and the standard of judgment is obvious: for *of course* it's better to have moral principles which are the true ones, or which are nearer to the true ones. And in fact, as has been suggested all along, the notion of moral progress is actually one of the strongest arguments for the realist view. If it really does make good sense to speak of moral progress and decline, and if it makes good sense *only* on the assumption that realism is true, then we have a short and sharp answer to the relativists.

We must ask, then, what happens if we reject the absolutist assumption, and assume instead that there is no single set of universal and immutable standards lying behind the actual standards; and since these are not the same everywhere and at all times, we have to select one particular set to judge by. In fact, of course, we use our own set. Now we normally use our standards of judgment to judge actions. But we can also use them to judge other standards. Take the first case, and recall what was said above about progress and decline in the matter of conformity between principle and practice. It is clear that this distinction still holds on a relativist view, and so the idea of progress and decline of this kind makes perfectly good sense. And so, of course, does the idea of moral effort.

But a difficulty arises when we turn to the other case, where we use our standards of judgment to judge other standards of judgment. We seem to have the following result, as a matter of pure logic: Any moral principle which is different from mine is necessarily wrong, by my standards. This is a matter of logic because of what we assumed in the code-comparing exercise: that a morality classifies actions into the required, the forbidden, and the permitted. Someone else's moral principle can differ from mine only if it classifies some actions differently. This means that some action which my principle forbids will be permitted or required by yours. But if my principle forbids it, then according to me the action is wrong; and any principle which permits or requires something wrong is itself wrong. So your principle is wrong, according to mine.

Now we come to the crucial question of change in standards. (Remember that we are no longer talking of change in our grasp or understanding of unchanging standards, but of changes in the standards themselves.) How shall I regard my own earlier standards, if they were different from the ones I now adopt? And how shall I think of possible future changes?

The answers must be, according to the same logic: My previous standards, if they were different from my present ones, were necessarily wrong. Therefore, necessarily, I have progressed. And still more remarkably: My future standards, if they are going to be different from my present ones, are necessarily going to be wrong. Therefore, necessarily, I cannot progress any further, but can only degenerate! (The same will apply if we read, instead of 'I', 'we' or 'our society' throughout.)

In other words, moral change between past and present is necessarily progressive, and moral change between present and future is necessarily retrogressive. But this is preposterous. We cannot possibly suppose ourselves to have proved, by pure logic, that, by an amazing coincidence, the present age happens to be the most morally enlightened of all time. Rather, all we have shown is an inevitable consequence of applying standards of judgment to themselves. Exactly the same consequences would follow in any other field of judgment: in art, religion, or even science and factual beliefs generally. If I used to believe in Father Christmas, but now believe in a rather different method of Christmas present distribution, I must necessarily believe my current belief to be progressive; and if I try to imagine myself coming to believe again in Father Christmas, I must necessarily think of this as a regrettable laspe into second childhood.

The point can be illustrated by the case of the young Russian nobleman discussed in some recent literature. This is a young man who knows that in middle age he will inherit great estates, and in his present youthful idealism he intends to give them away to the peasants. Yet he has every reason to think that when he does inherit, his moral principles will have changed to more conservative ones. He will then be condemning the follies of his youth; he will have progressed beyond them. Yet he cannot *now* think of that as progress. Bernard Williams, who discusses the case, tries to suggest that the later stage could be 'something now identified as a growth in enlightenment'.[20] But how can I identify a future belief as more enlightened than my present one, without *ipso facto* abandoning my present belief and adopting the other one, so that it is no longer a *future* belief?

We seem to have the result, then, that on a relativist view moral progress is either logically necessary or impossible. Since this is patently absurd, there must be something wrong with relativism. Does this drive us back to absolutism? Absolutism makes better sense of moral progress, yet it has its own problems, as we have seen.

The solution, inevitably, will be to abandon the sharp and simple contrast we have so far been working with, between an unqualified realism and an unqualified relativism. However, before seeing how this might be done, there is another possible line suggested by my brief allusion to science. Might it be possible to find a criterion for moral progress, independent of actual current moral standards, yet without invoking a set of absolutes? Science, for instance, is undoubtedly progressive, yet scientists seldom claim that this is a matter of approaching ever closer to a set of absolute truths about the universe. Why are we so sure that there has indeed been progress in science, and that this is not merely an illusion deriving from the logical fact that whatever our present beliefs are, we are bound, logically, to believe that they are true, and so better than those which have been discarded as false? Well, there is a further fact about new scientific theories compared with older ones, not just the fact that they are different. This is the fact that old theories are seldom actually rejected; more often the new ones *incorporate* the older ones. The new theories explain the same facts that the old ones explained, but some new facts as well, which the older theories could not explain. Thus Aristotle's theory of motion explains why stones fall to the ground, and so does Newton's; but Aristotle's theory doesn't explain the new fact that planets move in elliptical orbits, whereas Newton's does. It looks as if progress in science does have a certain marker. It is marked by theories becoming wider and more universal. Notice that this is a criterion *internal* to science. It is not a matter of saying that science is progressing because scientists are producing statements which are more true to nature; we cannot say that, because we have no independent access to nature by which we could check that the statements *are* more true or not. Universality is an internal fact about scientific theories.

Is there a similar internal progress-marker for morals? It seems at first sight that there is, and that it is this very same feature of greater universality. We can detect something analogous in changes of moral attitude over the ages. The ancient Greeks, for instance, had *different* moral codes for heroes and for lesser men; different codes for men and women; for free citizens and for slaves. The Stoics, followed by the early Christians, abolished some of these distinctions, moving towards a more universal human morality. And in more recent times there are movements campaigning for more equal consideration for women, for coloured immigrants, for future generations, for animals. All these movements are movements in the same direction: towards a widening of our moral concerns.

Unfortunately, this hope of finding a moral progress-marker, promising though it seems, is illusory. The comparison with science works in the opposite direction as well. The scientist's interest in the universal goes with a transcendence of the particular. Nothing in science depends on a particular object or event being that very individual; from the point of view of science, another such individual would do just as well. But in ethics an increasing concern for the general runs a serious risk of doing violence to the particular case; for ethics can *not* transcend the particularities of life; individuals are emphatically not substitutable for one another. Both Kantians and Utilitarians have a hard struggle on their hands to show that their theories do not involve this unwelcome treatment of the individual case, do not involve a disappearance of the notion of personal integrity, of what it is to be a person in relation to other persons (and including one's own past and future self). We shall return to this theme in Chapter X.

We return, then, to the suggestion of resolving the dilemma about realism and relativism in relation to moral progress, by softening up the contrast between the unqualified theory-types. The trouble with unqualified relativism is that it leads to an unacceptable 'Anything goes'. Not that *everything* is *permitted*, but that *anything* can be permitted or prescribed or prohibited. And the trouble with unqualified absolutism is that we find it very hard to accept that there is a set of moral truths 'out there' just waiting to be somehow grasped or approximated to. What we need is some intelligible link between principles of human conduct and *other* features of the human condition. This will help us to keep the best features of both contending theories. It will provide some sort of *grounding* for ethics, and so safeguard the appeal to objectivity and to something transcending personal and perhaps even social particularities. At the same time it will – or at least it can – allow for a sufficiently great variety of different codes, cultures, and ways of life, both actual and possible, and subject only to certain general constraints arising from the actual conditions of human life. Such an idea will be developed in the following chapter.

CHAPTER VII

Prescriptivism (2): Natural law

I introduced the term 'Prescriptivism' in Chapter V as a label for any kind of ethical theory that places such notions as rules, principles and verdicts at the centre of morality. It is a reminder that we are concerned to explain the essentially action-guiding function of morality, which cannot be at all adequately explained either by the traditional propositional or cognitive theories, or by the only other type of non-cognitive theory, namely emotivism. For the facts of the world, or even of another world, cannot, by themselves, constitute a moving appeal to action; while emotions are, notoriously, not so much guides as distractions.

Now the only field of human affairs which approximates to morality in its pervasiveness and generality, and where rules and principles of familiar kinds are operating, is the field of law; which is why I said that a prescriptivist type of theory is one which takes the legal analogy seriously. But although moral rules and principles are like legal ones in (at least) this respect of being pervasively action-guiding, we saw that there are also important differences. It is not clear exactly what moral rules are, what their content is, and what is their source, origin, or ground. In the last chapter we considered a pair of theory-types which have completely antagonistic answers to these questions. According to absolutism, the origin of moral rules is something immutable and transcendent, while according to relativism, moral rules are formulations of the actual, variable, and changing practices of different societies in different ages.

In this chapter I shall be considering an answer which avoids those extremes. This will be prescriptivism in the form of a natural law theory. Such a theory holds that the origin and ground of morality is to be found in the nature of man as a certain type of creature in a certain type of natural, terrestrial, environment.

To introduce the idea of natural law theory, let us begin by asking *how much* of morality we can expect to find a natural origin or basis for. It would be pretty absurd to suppose that any one particular detailed set of precepts – a specific positive morality – could be directly derived from some natural source. There is too much variation between different moral codes. This has been familiar to moral philosophers since antiquity; Aristotle explicitly notes, as something already long familiar, that, while fire burns both in Greece and in Persia, justice is not the same in both places. Some people, of course, have adopted a thoroughgoing relativism on the strength of these cultural variations. But a standard defence against unrestricted relativism is to appeal to (what I shall call) the Highest Common Factor view: that there is, and must be, something like a common core of content to all moralities that can be recognised *as* moralities. It is just not possible for anything whatever to be moral or immoral; there are certain constraints on what moral precepts can require or allow. Natural law theory is an attempt to establish what those constraints are, and what is the minimum common moral content that they generate.

Natural law is law which is neither man-made nor god-made. It is, however, capable of being formulated and understood by human beings, and of being assented to and accepted as a guide to conduct, by people who are able to reflect sufficiently deeply on their own nature and condition. As for a god, it is, equally, the law which any god who is concerned for the well-being of his creatures must necessarily wish them to observe (as John Stuart Mill said of Utilitarianism.)[21] The best modern exposition of this theory, in its secular version, is Professor Hart's, in his *Concept of Law*; but there is a surprisingly penetrating statement of the theory in Plato's dialogue *Protagoras*, which I shall quote more or less in full. It even includes the point about a god, which is not made by Hart. (The writing is deliberately allegorical, and the references to conventional gods are meant to be demythologised.)

> Men lived at first in scattered groups . . . They were devoured by wild beasts, since they were in all respects weaker . . . They sought to protect themselves by coming together and building fortified cities; but when they began to gather in communities they could not help injuring one another in their ignorance of the arts of co-operative living. Zeus, therefore, fearing the total destruction of the race, sent Hermes to impart to men the qualities of respect for others and a sense of justice . . . (Hermes asks whether justice and respect should be imparted unequally, like the skilled arts, or equally to all alike.) Equally (said Zeus). There could never be societies if only a few shared these virtues. Moreover, you must lay it down as my law that if anyone is found incapable of acquiring his share of these two virtues he shall be put to death as a disease in society.[22]

What makes this considerably more sophisticated than similar-looking versions by eighteenth-century Englishmen is that Protagoras makes it quite clear that the story about primitive men coming together in a 'social contract' is *only* a story, just as fictitious as those Homeric gods, and not implying for a moment that there ever actually was Hobbes's nasty brutish and short-lived savage (or Dryden's noble one).

Now for Hart. He agrees with Protagoras that the survival of human society is a necessary aim, and that this is a basic datum. 'Our concern is with social arrangements for continued existence, not with those of a suicide club.' He continues:

> We wish to know whether, among these social arrangements, there are some which may be illuminatingly ranked as *natural laws discoverable by reason*, and what their relation is to *human law and morality* . . . Reflection on some very obvious generalizations – indeed truisms – concerning human nature and the world in which men live, show that as long as these hold good, there are certain rules of conduct which any

social organization must contain *if it is to be viable*. Such rules do in fact constitute a common element in the *law and conventional morality* of all societies . . . where these are distinguished as different forms of social control. With them are found, both *in law and in morals*, much that is peculiar to a particular society and much that may seem arbitrary and a mere matter of choice. Such universally recognised principles of conduct which have a basis in elementary truths concerning human beings, their natural environment, and their aims, may be considered the *minimum content* of Natural Law.[23]

Notice five points in this passage:

(1) Hart constantly (three times in this quotation) brackets law with ('conventional') morality, meaning by morality here what I have been calling positive morality.

(2) Morality unqualified is then what Hart calls natural law, and it is the *common content* (highest common factor) both of the various positive moralities and of the various systems of law.

(3) We have not only a statement asserting that there is this common content, and telling us what it is; we also have an *explanation* of why it is what it is. (It is 'discoverable by reason'.)

(4) The explanation (or discovery) proceeds from two fundamental principles:

(a) that societies *survive* (They are not 'suicide clubs');

(b) that there are certain characteristic features of human beings as a species of organism on the earth, and certain features of our earthly environment, that we all share. (The 'truisms'.)

(5) The explanation (or discovery) takes the form of a demonstration that, given those features of human beings and the environment, human society *cannot survive unless* human beings accept certain constraints on their behaviour. These constraints are the rules of natural law. Given the truisms, natural law is a necessary condition of the survival of human society.

Now we come to the truisms themselves. First, what is meant by calling them truisms? Three things: (1) they are true; (2) they are self-evidently true; but (3) they may not be *obvious*, and so are worth stating.

The truisms which lead to Hart's 'minimum content of natural law' can be classified as biological, behavioural, and environmental. Hart lists five, but only two of these lead to any particular *content* in morals; the other three lead to various other features of morality which I will call 'formal' for the present. The two which lead to a specific content are these:

(i) 'Human Vulnerability' (Hart), to which, however, must be added a complementary feature, namely destructive power: a human capacity and readiness to hurt. This is then the truism that man is by nature capable of receiving, and of inflicting, serious bodily injury and death. And this is of course connected with the universally prevalent prohibitions on killing and injuring, except in closely specified circumstances. The necessity of the connection can be understood if we imagine a very different natural condition for man: if, for instance, we were heavily armour-plated, and so incapable of being damaged; or if we were immobile, like plants, and so incapable of wielding weapons or moving to attack. Rules against killing or maiming might still exist in these altered conditions, but they would no longer be *necessary*.

(ii) 'Limited Resources' (Hart). The fact that the basic necessities of life are always in short supply makes inevitable some form of property institution (not necessarily, of course, an individualist or capitalist property system), together with a set of rules governing the exchange of property, that is, contracts and promises. Again, the necessity of this can be understood by imagining natural conditions in which human beings never needed to labour to produce and conserve their resources in order to survive: if, for instance, they could extract their food from the air (again, like the lilies of the field).

I will mention more briefly Hart's other truisms since they do not lead to any particular content: (iii) 'Approximate Equality' (no man is enormously stronger than another) which makes generally acceptable a common system of mutual forbearances and compromise. (Morality does not operate between nations, just because nations are not even approximately equal; and it operates very imperfectly in political relations, for the same reason: as in the case of electoral promises.) (iv) 'Limited Altruism' (men are not devils, but neither are they angels) explains the necessity of restraints, and at the same time their possibility; (v) 'Limited Understanding and Strength of Will' makes it necessary to apply sanctions, including here the informal sanctions of moral disapproval, as an artificial incentive to conformity for those whose own reason or self-control are insufficient.

Before we come to the evaluation of natural law theory, let me allow it to comprise the doctrine of Human Rights – a matter of considerable controversy today, especially in international politics. Human rights and natural law are closely connected, in fact they are both aspects of the same thing. If there *are* any human rights, they will have to be rights which we have simply because of our nature as members of the human species, not rights which we have *conferred* on us by particular societies or institutions (such as British citizenship, or membership of the University of St Andrews). But since it is our *nature* to be members of our species, these human rights will be natural rights. Now what is it to have a right? Very roughly, to say that A has a right to X means that people ought to let A have X, or ought not to prevent his having it. These look like laws. So natural rights will be conferred by natural laws. And if we look at any actual list of (real or alleged) human rights, we shall in fact find a close correspondence between them and something like the list of natural laws we have just been considering. Laws against killing and stealing correspond exactly to the Right to Life and Right to Property.

In evaluating the theory of natural law, we must be careful to see just what it is claiming. In one respect its claims are quite modest, in another quite ambitious. It is modest in scope, because it is explicitly concerned only with what it calls the *minimum* content of morality; as far as we have seen, it seems to be restricted to rules governing matters of life and death, injury, property and contracts. Further, these rules are all *prohibitive*: there is no positive inducement to act in virtuous ways, only inhibitions against wrongdoing. The morality of the Good Samaritan is not catered for. Thirdly, only *primary* rules are dealt with; nothing is said about those special circumstances in which it may be permissible, or even mandatory, to destroy life, inflict bodily harm, deprive of possession or break a promise; and all or most of these things are generally held to be sometimes morally justifiable.

[101]

The reasons for these limitations are fairly obvious. The first limitation – the restricted range of topics – is explained by the fact that only one basic aim, that of survival, is considered. (Even this concept was one of *social*, not individual, survival, as we see from the end of the quotation from Plato's *Protagoras*. But the two are sufficiently close for me to ignore the distinction in what follows.) So any moral rules which are not directly concerned with survival will not be covered. And this is exactly what we should expect; after all, survival is the *basic* aim, because if this aim is not achieved, no others can be. Only survivors can be Samaritans. But it is quite open to the natural law theorist to introduce other, less basic aims, to explain other areas of moral control – and still remain within the area of universally recognised principles, rather than regional variations. An obvious case would be the moral (and legal) controls on mating and procreation. It is noticeable that there are no sexual restraints in Hart's list, even though such restraints are in fact universal in all societies. The reason why they are not in Hart's list is because such things as sexual promiscuity, incest, or adultery, are not *obviously* incompatible with survival, as promiscuous killing would be. As a matter of interest, in passing, we might well ask what basic aim, second only to survival, *is* promoted by the rules governing mating. One suggestion might be that this aim is concerned with *identity*. Why is identity so important? Well, given that the most important thing for me as an individual is that I should survive, the next most important thing is that I should survive as a person who knows who he is; and this would seem to be impossible without some specific kinship system and the rules built into it. To illustrate both points – the peculiar awfulness of flawed identity, and the absolute necessity for kinship rules – consider a classic example of what happens when things go wrong: the Oedipus story. One of the most horrifying moments in Sophocles's tragedy is where we share Oedipus's realisation of the plight of his children by Jocasta: Antigone doesn't know whether she is his daughter or his sister, because she is both.[24] As regards the kinship rules, here again, as in the case of property, it doesn't have to be any particular kinship system, such as ours; the regional variations are enormous.[25]

The second limitation – to prohibitions rather than recommendations – is the negative aspect of law, and of much of morality, which we have already discussed. Again it is obvious that a basic aim like survival *is* promoted by bare abstentions, whereas a more positive and sophisticated aim, like becoming a doctor, obviously cannot be promoted by *not* doing things. And there may well be areas of morality which *are* linked with positive aims, and so cannot be dealt with by natural law theory.

The third limitation – to primary rules, with no account of the necessary exceptions and qualifications – is to be explained in the same way. A primary rule against killing is necessary for survival; but a total ban is not. But the aims to be secured by particular exemptions from the killing ban are too many and too various to be included in a simple theory.

Our next question is this. Given that there is *some* connection between the truisms about human nature and the minimum content of morality, just what is this connection? Here the claims of natural law theory are quite ambitious. Hart wants the rules to be 'discoverable by human reason'. This means that the truisms must both *explain*, and *justify*, the rules. It is important to see that these are different claims. As Hart himself points out, an explanation alone might be a merely causal explanation. There could well *be* a causal connection between the truisms and the rules, just as (at the level of regional variations) there just could be a causal link between, say, specific methods of child-weaning in a particular society, and, say, a certain puritanical streak in the moral code of that society. It could be just an empirical fact that societies with those weaning methods developed that kind of puritanism. There might even be psychological mechanisms to explain the connection. But these facts would not *justify* those attitudes. Causal explanation is a matter of external factors affecting things, or affecting people, without their thinking about them; but justification involves people doing some thinking, the result of which may or may not coincide with the products of the causal process. So, in the case of our truisms and the content of moral rules about killing and so on, we have two distinct claims. Let us take each in turn.

First, is there a causal connection? Well, there obviously is. To see this, let us imagine a collection of artefacts in the form of humanoid machines (used, perhaps, for large-scale automated excavation work). These powerful machines are easily capable of damaging one another, but they are equipped with special circuits or programmes which prevent this from happening most of the time. Now this electronic gadgetry would then explain, in purely causal terms, why the machines do not quickly end up in the scrap-yard. Similarly, if we look at people from the outside, as it were, we can explain why *they* do not quickly end up in the grave-yard, by referring to their built-in, programmed ethical behaviour-patterns.

As far as causal explanation goes, then, Hart, and even Protagoras, are unquestionably right. In fact natural law theory conforms quite well to the standard pattern of scientific explanation, and is duly verified. Given certain theoretical assumptions – first, what we might call the appropriate Conservation Law, that human society does tend to conserve itself, and, second, given that the salient features of human nature and the human environment are such and such, it can be deduced what patterns of behaviour they must be adopting – if they were to adopt any other pattern, they would not be conserved. Then we apply the empirical test, by looking to see if actual human beings in societies do have rules against killing, maiming, stealing and fraud. This then confirms the theory, which then constitutes an explanation of the facts – the facts in this case being the basic moral rules.

But what of the second claim? Does the theory *justify* the moral rules, as well as explaining them? To answer this, we have to stop looking at people from the outside, like the humanoid machines, and think of them in the way we think of ourselves, as having an inner life as well, capable of reflecting on our nature and condition, on possible aims and goals, and possible ways of achieving them; and to justify the rules we shall have to see that they are a way, perhaps the only way, of achieving a continued life, or a life worth continuing. In other words, we shall be concerned not with causes but with reasons. The truisms do explain the rules, but we want to know whether they justify them. And I shall suggest that the theory's justificatory power is very small indeed.

[104]

I think there are three distinct ways in which it falls short.

(1) The theory will only justify certain rather abstract, general features of any actual moral code. There are justifiably rules against killing, stealing and so on; but the actual rules of the system, taken as they stand, may well be unjustifiable. They may indeed promote survival; but it may well be that survival in a particular social context is secured only by an inhumane or even inhuman system. However, this is an inevitable limitation of the theory.

(2) Another limitation is this. Suppose the theory does amply justify people *collectively* obeying the rules, in that there is a very good reason why they (collectively) should. Yet does it justify each and every individual in obeying the rules? Does it provide him or her with a good and sufficient reason why he or she should conform? Obviously it provides you with *some* reason, since *in* conforming you are helping to stabilise and confirm the system of rules on which your security depends. But is this a *sufficient* reason? Suppose you can gain great benefits for yourself by breaking the rules, by going in for crime, while still retaining the protection of society? Won't you gain more that way? Well, most of us are deterred by the sanctions, legal and moral, imposed for that very purpose. But suppose you are very powerful, or very clever, or both, and you can evade or disregard the sanctions? Why shouldn't you cash in on the benefits of a secure society, which depends on other people keeping to the rules, while you yourself opt out? Or, to put it another way, isn't the best possible life the life of the thoroughgoing egoist in a society of thoroughgoing altruists? This is very much the position that Plato's Thrasymachus adopted. It took Plato the whole of the *Republic* to work out an answer and few people are convinced that his answer is completely satisfactory. The question is, indeed, the most difficult one there is for ethical theory. It is the question 'Why should *I* be moral?', 'Why should *I* observe any standards of conduct whatever?' We shall meet this question again later.

(3) So natural law theory fails to justify morality to the individual, at least if he is a thoroughgoing egoist. But even if he is not – even if he is the opposite extreme, a thoroughly conscientious, altruistic, even saintly, moralist – the natural law theory may still

fail to justify *his* morality. In an extreme case he may regard survival as totally irrelevant; he may even see a clear duty of self-immolation, or even a mission to destroy his society (as, some have held, Jesus and his early followers did). Or, again, survival, though not irrelevant, may rank so low on his list of moral values that the 'minimum content' of the natural law theory is, for him, minimal indeed and far outweighed by other things.

According to these last two criticisms, then, it is a defect of natural law theory that it deals only with the external aspects of morality, and entirely overlooks the point of view of the individual agent and thinker, whether he is an egoist or a sincere moralist. It has nothing to say about the phenomena of moral choice or decision, or on what it is to make up one's mind on a moral issue. This is the point of departure for modern prescriptivism, as we shall see when we come to Professor Hare; it is also a starting-point for a much earlier prescriptivist, Immanuel Kant; and for much of the thinking of the Continental Existentialists. But first we must deal, however briefly, with the unfinished business about morals and religion.

CHAPTER VIII

Morals and religion

This interlude for theology will necessarily be a very brief and schematic treatment of a very complex subject. I shall ignore as far as possible the formidable questions of religious knowledge, such as the question whether, and how, we can know that there is a God; but I shall not be able to avoid altogether one question about religious knowledge: given that God does require certain things of us, how can we know what they are? My main question will be this. Given that it is the will of some God – and for the sake of argument let it be the God of the Christians, Jews and Moslems – that we should behave in certain roughly specifiable ways: what reasons, if any, could we have for behaving in those ways, reasons which we would *not* have if we did *not* believe that God had willed them?

Let me start by going back to the classic statement by David Hume:

In every system of morality which I have hitherto met with, I have always remarked, that the author proceeds for some time in the ordinary way of reasoning, and establishes the being of a God, or makes observations concerning human affairs; when of a sudden I am surprised to find, that instead of the usual copulations of propositions, *is* and *is not*, I meet with no proposition that is not connected with an *ought*, or *ought not* . . . But as this *ought*, or *ought not*, expresses some new relation or affirmation, it is necessary that it should be observed and explained; and that a reason should be given, for what seems altogether inconceivable, how this new relation can be a deduction from the others, which are entirely different from it.[26]

As far as God and his relation to ethics are concerned, Hume's challenge can be stated thus: what logical relation can there be between the claim that God exists, and that he requires us to do or not to do certain things – between that and the claim that *we ought* to do those things? On the face of it this looks like an invalid inference from a fact to a value. More formally, from the factual statement that something is the case, you cannot infer a normative statement that something ought to be the case. This is because of the familiar logical principle that there cannot be anything in the conclusion of an inference that was not contained in the premises. Here we have something normative (as expressed by 'ought') in the conclusion, but not in the premises. Any such conclusion must therefore be just as invalid as a conclusion about crocodiles in an argument where crocodiles are not mentioned in any of the premises.

Well, it is true that we can never deduce an 'ought' from an 'is'? Let us test this by looking at an apparent exception. Take the inference: 'It's going to rain, so you ought to take your umbrella'. (It does not matter whether or not this is a moral 'ought'.) This inference is invalid according to the standard formula, but in fact it is obviously all right, because we know that we are meant to supply certain other premises which are too obvious to be worth stating ('If it rains and you haven't got an umbrella, you will get wet'; and 'You ought not to let yourself get wet'.) Notice that one of these hidden premises is indeed normative, as the principle requires. The upshot of this, then, is, in the case of God and morality: if an 'ought'-judgment is to be backed by reasons, at least one reason must be a normative one. But *is* the existence of God, or the fact that he requires us to do this or that, a normative reason? Apparently not. The difficulty here is commonly stated in the form of this dilemma: 'Given that it is right to do X, and that it is God's will that we should do X: is X right because God wills it, or does God will it because it is right?' The classic statement of this problem is the *Euthyphro* dilemma in Plato's dialogue of that name.

One classic solution is that of William of Ockham. Take this solution first: X is right because God wills it. We now have the formally invalid argument from a factual to a normative statement: F/N. We can restore validity in two ways. One way would be to delete the N-element in the conclusion. The other way would be to add an N-element to the premiss, as we have just seen. Take the first way. Here we shall be left with no conclusion at all, unless we simply write the premiss again; this will be formally valid, and represents the statement 'God wills X because he wills X'. On this it might seem more than enough to comment (a) that it is an empty tautology; and (b) that we have made the inference valid only by taking away the very thing that made it important: the normative element of 'right'. But there are two more things worth saying, in view of what is to come: (c) the new formula raises the question 'Could God have willed anything other than X?' It certainly seems unsatisfactory to say that God wills what he wills, with the implication that he could have willed just anything, including the opposite of X, which is presumptively wrong. Further, (d) the formula makes it impossible for there to be rational *praise* of God; we can only praise someone, even God, by submitting his activities, as it were, to an independent tribunal, and finding that they satisfy the required conditions.

As an example of this problem in real (or at least terrestrial) life: I once read in the newspaper that a certain change was to be made in the regulations governing the award of the Oxford Doctorate.[27] Originally there had been the rule 'The thesis must satisfy the examiners that it is a substantial contribution to learning and suitable for publication'; and this was to be amended to 'The thesis must satisfy the examiners that it is worthy of the award of the degree of Ph.D.' Now if we take this literally, and deliberately ignore our background knowledge of the total probity and expertise of the Oxford examiners, what this amounts to is this: the examiners think a thesis is worthy of the degree because they think it is worthy of the degree. The analogy with the divine will is obvious.

But of course we cannot, and should not, in practice ignore our background knowledge about the examiners; and in religious practice, too, we cannot, and should not, ignore what we know about God. And one thing we presumably know about him is that he is perfectly good. (This is the point where I said the question of religious knowledge could not be altogether avoided.) God only wills things which are good, and forbids just those things which are evil. In terms of our original dilemma: God wills X because X is right. This meets all the objections to the barren tautology that God wills what he wills. (a) We no longer have a tautology, but a substantial assertion that God's will coincides with what is right and good; (b) we have not lost the normative force of 'ought'; (c) we no longer have an open question whether God could have willed just anything: he cannot; not because he is not omnipotent, but because it would be contrary to his own divine nature, which is supremely good; and (d) we can again rationally praise God, for his goodness.

However, we have a heavy price to pay for all this. We have restored validity to the formally invalid F/N inference, not this time by deleting the N-element in the conclusion, but by adding an N-element to the premiss. And although we are now able to make interesting and substantial remarks about God's will – namely that it conforms to the standards of the right and good – we have only landed up with another tautology in a different place, namely where our duty is located. God wills X because it is right; but it is right only because it is right. As far as our duty is concerned, God's will has dropped right out of the inference. In relation to ethics, God's will is an unnecessary intermediary. So, the conclusion emerges that ethics can indeed be of service to theology, by throwing some light on the essential nature of God; but theology cannot have any relevance to ethics; at least, it cannot provide us with any reasons for acting which we do not already have, apart of course from eschatological reasons such as hopes of reward and threats of punishment, which however are mere sanctions, appeals to self-interest and not to anything that could properly be called religious.

Much the same conclusion was reached by Immanuel Kant, and I would like to re-state the argument in a more Kantian way. Kant claimed to find a 'crude circularity' in attempts to base ethics on the will of a supreme being. God wills that we act in certain ways, namely those we now call good. If this proposition is 'synthetic', that is not a mere tautology, then it must be at least logically possible that God could have willed quite other kinds of behaviour, including those we now call evil. But a god who willed such behaviour would not be a fitting object of worship; that is, he could not *be* God. Even a god of whom it was logically possible that he might will evil behaviour could not be accepted as worthy of worship. Worshippers can settle for nothing less than a God who is *necessarily* good. This is the 'crude circularity' of which Kant complains: claiming to define good in terms of God, only to find that God has to be defined in terms of good.

Nor does Kant hesitate to spell out the devastating implications for theology of this idea that the very nature of God must depend on what we as worshippers find acceptable in the light of our human morality. Kant has, in his metaphysical works, maintained that, in a certain important sense, Nature is man-made; in his ethical works he maintains that morality is man-made; and now he has to conclude that even God is man-made:

> Much as my words may startle you, you must not condemn me for saying: every man creates his God. From the moral point of view . . . you even have to create your God, in order to worship in Him your creator. For in whatever way . . . the Deity should be made known to you – even . . . if He should reveal Himself to you, it is you . . . who must judge whether you are permitted (by your conscience) to believe in Him and to worship Him.[28]

Similarly, to switch to a moral philosopher whose views are usually seen as diametrically opposed to Kant's, John Stuart Mill says of his own doctrine of Utilitarianism, 'We need a doctrine of ethics . . . to *interpret* to us the will of God.'[29]

A final version of the dilemma might be: is God the author of the moral law, or is he subject to it? There seem to be insuperable objections to both possibilities. An interesting alternative, and surely the only one left, is to hold that God and the moral law are in some fundamental sense identical. We should then have a moral pantheism, like the metaphysical pantheism of Spinoza: God would be identical with both aspects of the Universe. Kant comes very near to such a view when in a famous passage he speaks of two things which above all else fill the human heart with awe, reverence – the sense of being in the presence of the divine – namely, 'the starry heavens above, and the moral law within'. In the starry heavens we see and revere one aspect of God, in the moral law we see and revere another.[30]

This must end our religious interlude; but notice that much of what I have been saying about a divine authority for morals would apply with equal force to the idea of any human authority. There can be no such thing as a moral authority, whether divine or human – if by 'authority' is meant that one being can be an authority over another. No one can have authority in matters of right and wrong, except in that special sense in which a man can be his own authority, or as Conscience (suitably interpreted) can be. This is the idea of moral autonomy, which belongs to pre-scriptivism proper.

CHAPTER IX

Prescriptivism (3): Rational autonomy

(i)

We saw in the chapter on 'natural law theory' that this omits the point of view of the individual moralist; and we saw in the chapter on 'Morals and Religion' that a theology-based ethics also seemed (to Kant, at least) to leave no room for the freedom of the moral agent. There has been a powerful stream of thought in the history of ethics since the Middle Ages which emphasises this essential freedom of the moral agent. The high water marks in this stream of thought have been Kant, and the Existentialist movement, with a neo-Kantian development in the work of Professor R.M. Hare, who says, for instance: 'We are free to form our own moral opinions in a much stronger sense than we are free to form our own opinions as to what the facts are'.[31]

Kant's greatest achievement in ethical theory was a synthesis of this extreme individualism with the extreme universalism (as we might call it) of an appeal to objective reason as something common to, and indeed transcending, all men. Here we begin to see how the obstructive contrast between the subjective and the objective is to be superseded by a grasp of their joint necessity. What is common to all (objective) must nevertheless be open to individual acceptance or rejection (subjective). Hare, too, wants a synthesis of these two elements, as summed up in the title of his second book, *Freedom and Reason*. It matters that a person makes his own decisions; yet it also matters that he make the right decisions.

Kant was fighting a war on two fronts. The individualist part of his doctrine is a reaction against theories which attempt to base ethics on a natural, or supernatural, order of things. His universalism, on the other hand, is a reaction against the wrong sort of individualism: the sort we have already touched on in discussing emotivism, and which was associated, historically, with the philosophy of David Hume, who was generally regarded as Kant's chief adversary. One of Hume's most celebrated remarks is that reason is the slave of the passions. Another is: 'Morality is more properly felt than judged of'. And here is one of his arguments to prove that ethics is based on emotion and not reason. Consider an oak tree, which produces an acorn, which germinates, grows, overshadows, and finally kills the parent tree. Translate this into human terms, and you have an example, not just of murder, but of matricide, one of the deadliest of sins. Yet there is nothing sinful in the oak-tree case. So there is a big difference to be explained, why one is a case of morality and the other is not. Can we find this difference by exercising our reason? No, says Hume, because the exercise of reason will be a matter of comparing, analysing, abstracting, and can only tell us that the cases are indeed alike. So the difference must be a case of what we *feel* about the two cases, since it cannot be a case of what we *know* about them. And the difference is, of course, that a person killing his parent excites very strong feelings in us, whereas a tree killing another tree does not.

Now who are the *we* in whom this killing excites these feelings? All men, or just some? In this particular case, no doubt it would be true to say that virtually all men would have feelings of horror; but even if they all did, it would be in no sense a necessary truth that they must have this kind of feeling. It would just be a brute fact that people happened to feel that way. There would be nothing irrational about feeling differently. And if men do formulate moral principles to the effect that killing is wrong, and that killing parents is especially wrong, this is not because killing parents *is* wrong; it is merely a convenient reminder about how people are likely to feel and to react.

[114]

All this is totally unacceptable to Kant, who rejects it at every point. To begin with the last point: Kant insists that the relation between how people feel and whether things are wrong is exactly the opposite: it is not that things are wrong because people feel the way they do, on the contrary people feel the way they do, they experience feelings of horror or revulsion, because the things are *wrong*. And (working back through the other points), it *is* deeply irrational for someone to have no reaction, or a favourable reaction, to moral offences; it is not a brute fact that people feel the way they do, because these feelings are a response to what reason reveals to be unacceptable conduct; and finally, whatever reason reveals is a *necessary* truth, which could not be otherwise.

I said that emotivism is the wrong sort of individualism. (I leave aside the question whether Hume's emotivism has been properly interpreted.) Let us first get clear how it *is* a form of individualism, and then why it is the wrong sort. It is a form of individualism because emotion, by contrast with reason, seems to suggest a specific emotional state for each person, while reason is necessarily common and universal. A person's emotional reaction to a situation is typically different from that of another person; and it could be argued that the totality of his felt experience is inevitably different from everybody else's. Now when I use my reason to understand something, say the theorem of Pythagoras (the proposition, not the proof), my rational understanding of this item of knowledge about triangles and squares is exactly the same as yours. If it were not, one of us would not *be* understanding *the* theorem. Every exercise of reason is necessarily, because of the very nature of reason, the same for everyone. But when I react emotionally to something – say a piece of music, a piece of news, or even the theorem of Pythagoras again (we can have emotional reactions even to bits of geometry), my emotional reaction is *not* the same as yours, or anyone else's. If it were, in all cases, we could hardly *be* different persons. In short, reason assimilates, makes us one, whereas emotion individuates, keeps us apart. And since emotion *is* so closely bound up with individuality, while reason is not, it is not surprising that an ethical individualist – someone who wants to do justice to the role of the

[115]

individual in ethics – should be tempted by an emotivist theory.

If we now ask why emotivism is the wrong sort of individualism, the answer has already been given in our earlier discussion in Chapter IV (p.54), when I pointed out that emotivism, in failing to distinguish between feelings and values, or in attempting to reduce the one to the other, simply ignored a major feature of moral thinking: namely universality and the idea of moral commitment. My moral views commit me to regrets about past misdeeds, whatever I may have felt, or even thought, at the time, and even if I thought at the time that they were right; and my moral views also commit me to having certain intentions in the future, irrespective of what I may be feeling or thinking then; and my moral views commit me to having obligations to people, or to making judgments about people, whom I have never even heard of, and so cannot possible have feelings about.

But these universality features force us to recognise an essential place for reason in morality. What, then, happens to the individual? Well, there is still an essential place for him too, and it is to Kant's credit that he reconciled these two apparently conflicting factors. Even in the field of theoretical reason, such as mathematics and the physical sciences, the products of this reasoning are not bits of the fabric of the universe which we happen to stumble across. Pythagoras didn't discover the theorem that bears his name, in the sense in which Abel Tasman discovered New Zealand. Such things are in an important sense created – one might even say invented – by men; and they are maintained in being, given a continuing life, by men. And both sorts of activity are activities of individuals; not only the brilliant achievements of intellectual pioneers like Pythagoras and Newton, but also the more humdrum achievements of ordinary people like ourselves who apply our reason to understanding, verifying and justifying to ourselves the theoretical discoveries of greater minds. Everyone who works through the proof of a theorem, or a simple logical exercise, and *sees* that the result is what it is, is exercising individual responsibility and commitment. This is what distinguishes him from the plagiarist (or the parrot) who just copies something. (And even the visitor to New

Zealand sees for himself, as opposed to just repeating a geography lesson.)

The same will hold good, *a fortiori*, of practical reason. If there are principles of good conduct, awaiting 'discovery' by human reason, then those who discover them will have vindicated the individuality of moral thinking. They will be the great moral teachers and reformers. But individuality does not stop there. Any ordinary moral thinker, at least if he is sincere, will also have acted as a free individual agent. We do not need to be reformers or pioneers; anyone who *adopts* a moral view, as opposed to blindly following one, or just doing what he is told, is exercising his individuality. There is again a difference between originality and plagiarism, even when the outward result is the same.

This synthesis of reason and individualism is embodied in Kant's famous formula of the Categorical Imperative: you are to act in such a way that you can will a universal imperative that everyone should act in the same way. This sounds rather like a form of the Golden Rule (Do unto others as you would they do to you). But this is totally rejected by Kant, because it appeals to wants, which are in the same class as emotions, and not to reason. Yet at the same time it does appeal to what you, the individual moral thinker or agent, are to decide for yourself.

In what way is Kant's own formula an appeal to reason? Well, because what you 'can' or 'cannot' will is supposed to be a matter of logic. Kant thinks that any immoral action is such that we logically cannot will that everyone should do it, and that this illogicality makes it immoral. Now there certainly are actions which we logically cannot will. For example, we cannot will that even one person should make a round square. And although we can will that one person should win a race, we logically cannot will that everyone should win the race. Unfortunately, Kant's attempts to show, by means of examples, that immoral actions do involve contradictions of this kind, when universalised, are not very successful. His most plausible example is the case of making a false promise. There *is* something very close to a logical inconsistency in the idea of everyone making promises which they do not intend to keep: surely there could not *be* promises in those conditions, so we seem to be saying that there is and there isn't a

[117]

promise. The concept of promising is a very complex moral concept, and rather than pursue it here I prefer to change the example slightly, to a lying statement. The action here, which is supposed to be immoral, is: saying something you don't believe with the intention that the person addressed will believe it. If we try to universalise this, we see at once a sort of contradiction. If we say 'Everyone is to say things they don't believe with the intention that everyone is to believe them', we are envisaging a situation in which no one will believe what anyone says, and so no one can even form the intention that people will believe what he says. So the whole idea of making statements, including lying statements, in those conditions becomes self-defeating. So far Kant seems to be right. But even if he were successful in the case of promising or truth-telling, he certainly isn't in his other examples. Take suicide, for instance. Kant seems to be saying that suicide is wrong because universalised suicide would amount to the destruction of the human race. What is the contradiction here? Between the idea of a person committing suicide, and there being no longer any persons around to do so? That would be too absurd; and in any case Kant is relying on underlying metaphysical assumptions about the purpose of life. But there is still a fallacy in the argument. There is a confusion over what legislation requires and what it *permits*. If I intend to commit suicide, and to do so on principle, as Kant requires, the principle on which I act will not be one which *requires* me (and everyone else) to commit suicide, but only one which *allows* me to, or does *not* require me not to. And there is no shadow of contradiction in the idea of everybody being *allowed* to commit suicide.

To sum up Kant's contribution to prescriptivism: Kant's ethical theory makes one vital and, I think, successful claim, and one which is less successful (but in fact less important). First, every man is his own moralist; everyone's conscience is his own ultimate authority; and this is the only kind of moral authority there can be. Second, there is what appears to be a list of (some of the) actual demands that conscience, as the voice of reason, does make of us. The first claim is successful, the second one only partly so. It is unsuccessful in spelling out a detailed manual of duties; but it is doubtful if Kant really intended it to do that. But it is successful in giving life and colour to the first claim: in making clearer what is involved in taking up a moral attitude of any kind, in taking part in a moral way of life. We can see how it does this if we look at two other formulations that Kant gives of the same Categorical Imperative. One is: Always regard every man as an end in himself, and never use any man merely as a means to your own ends. The third version is: Always act as both sovereign and subject in a kingdom of ends. The third formula describes an ideal community of beings, all subject to the moral law, but each of them at the same time a sovereign legislator, because he freely and responsibly makes that law his own. The second formula emphasises respect for persons as a necessary ingredient in the moral outlook. Both of them have had important practical influences in the subsequent history of liberalism and Western democracy.

(ii)

Modern prescriptivism is usually associated with the work of Professor R.M. Hare, whose book *The Language of Morals*, with its successors, *Freedom and Reason* and *Moral Thinking*, is widely regarded as the most important ethical work of its time, and it is central to any discussion of modern moral philosophy.

Like Kant, Hare achieves a synthesis of the individualist and universalist features of morality (epitomised in the second title); and, again like Kant, he tends to suggest that much of the actual content of morality can be derived from the idea of pure practical reason. (It turns out to be strongly Utilitarian.) What he does is to develop a precise theory of what is involved in being moral: in having moral principles, or a moral attitude, or in making moral evaluations, of whatever kind; a theory which is entirely free of all presuppositions, metaphysical or theological, except only for the idea of man as a creature capable of decision-making; more strictly, decisions about his own actions. (We see at once that this will remedy the deficiency we noted in Natural Law theory (p.106), that it omits the element of decision-making.) A theory which confines itself to this – to Kant's first claim only – is inevitably open to some seemingly obvious objections: for instance, that it implies, unacceptably, that anything whatever could be thought right or wrong, or could even *be* right or wrong; or that a person just chooses what moral principles to adopt. We shall see later how prescriptivism can meet this, and several other, objections. Let us first see briefly how Hare develops his formal theory of what makes moral discourse moral. (This will constitute a reply to the central question of ethical theory, as raised on p.34 and p.73.)

Hare starts from the premiss that the primary function of moral language is to guide conduct. (This, we remember, was one of the criteria that any satisfactory ethical theory had to meet: as we have seen, it is a virtue of prescriptivism that it makes this the primary criterion.) Again like Kant, Hare speaks of imperatives. He develops a logic of the imperative mood to set alongside the more conventional logic of the indicative mood. The primary function of sentences in the indicative mood is to provide answers to questions of the form 'What is the case?', and the answer takes the form of a *statement*, which is true or false. The primary function of the imperative mood is to answer questions of the form 'What shall I do?'. What form does this answer take?

There are very many ways of answering questions of this form, and, correspondingly, many varieties of imperative. There are the imperatives of advice, warning, direct commands, requests, prayers, suggestions, threats; some of these need not be grammatically imperative at all (Hare shows this with a convincing example: a very effective way of getting a man to take off his trousers is to tell him that a scorpion has just crawled up his trouser leg – an urgent warning or advice is grammatically indicative, but functionally imperative). Now here are *moral* imperatives to be singled out from this variety? Clearly there must be an important difference between moral advice (say) and other kinds. If someone asks me to advise him how to succeed in embezzling some public funds, I might be able to give him some technical advice (if I am a professional accountant, say), but I cannot give him moral advice, since the only advice I could give him from a moral point of view would be: 'Don't do it at all'. This is the difference, of course, that Kant marked by his distinction between the Hypothetical and the Categorical Imperative.

Hare arrives at the special features of the moral imperative by noting that all the other forms of imperative are relativized to particularities of place, time, and persons. A straight command or request (like 'Shut the door') involves several such particularities: it is issued by a particular speaker to a particular hearer, and it requires a particular action,[32] which itself will usually involve a particular place and a particular time. Some of these particularities can be eliminated; for example, if a dictator issues a law, the particular hearer and the particular action are replaced by the generality of subject people and their actions in general; but there is still the particular utterer who issues the rule, the rule-*r*. Hare's claim is that when *all* the particularities have been eliminated, we shall have a truly universal imperative, and this universal imperative is identical with a moral principle. All moral principles are basically of the form 'Everyone, always, is to X', or 'No one, ever, is to Y' – whatever actions X and Y may be, whoever the agent may be, and whoever the utterer may be. How do these general imperatives get brought to bear on particular people and their actions? The connection between theory and practical conduct is this: in practice we say things like 'Your action, A, was wrong'. This means, according to Hare, 'In doing A, you acted contrary to a principle, that is, a universal imperative, to which I hereby subscribe'.

The expression 'hereby subscribe' is meant to capture the double relation of a moral agent with a moral principle, which Kant so strongly emphasised with his somewhat metaphorical talk of sovereign and subject. A moral principle, though purified of all reference to particulars, has all the same got to attach itself, as it were, to particular agents, if it is ever to be effective. The moral agent gets himself attached to it, in Hare's terms, by *subscribing* to it. That is, he both regards himself as subject to it (he allows it to control his actions), and he actively endorses it, takes responsibility for it (he would control other people's actions by it, as well as his own). Note the word 'subject' there, and the word 'subscribe': the 'sub' reminds us of the connection with subjectivity.[33]

Going back to the variety of imperatives, we can now see how moral advice, say, differs from other kinds. Advice of any kind differs from a straight command or request, in that it involves

[121]

reasons. I do not need reasons when commanding or requesting (of course I shall normally *have* a reason, but a command without a reason does not thereby cease to be a command); but I do need reasons when advising, and I must necessarily — by a necessity of reason —have the same reasons if different people in similar circumstances ask me for advice. If someone asks me for advice on gardening: 'Should I sow my broad beans in the autumn or in the spring?', and I say 'In the autumn'; if he goes on to ask 'Why do you advise autumn rather than spring?' and I say 'For no reason at all, I just think you should sow them in the autumn', he is entitled to complain that I am not giving him advice at all. Advice is advice only if it is backed up by reasons: in this case, for instance, that autumn-sown beans are less likely to be attacked by certain pests. And if someone else asks me the same question, I am logically bound to give him the same advice, based on the same reason.

Moral advice, then, being advice, must be backed by reasons, which will be moral reasons; and just as my gardening advice was backed by a quite general proposition, without reference to particularities, so my moral advice has to be backed by something quite general and unparticularised. And this can only be some universal principle. But there is a crucial difference between what backs up the technical advice, and what backs up the moral advice. The technical backing is *informative* (beans just are susceptible to the pests) while the moral backing is *normative* or prescriptive (everyone is to X). This is as it should be, since all advice other than moral advice is a case of take-it-or-leave-it. The facts of the world do not, of themselves, dictate any one course of action rather than another. A piece of non-moral advice only comes into play, as it were, when it connects with what someone happens to want. My gardening advice is effective only if, in addition to being backed by something true, it also corresponds with what my questioner wants. I assumed, of course, that he wanted to raise a good crop of beans. But that was only an assumption. He *might* want to engineer a spectacular failure (perhaps to persuade his wife that it wasn't worth while trying to grow beans). This is what Kant meant by the hypothetical imperative. But moral advice is never a case of take-it-or-leave-it, depending on what the listener happens to want. It is meant to be taken whatever he happens to want. This is why the reasons backing moral advice can never be solely statements of fact, like the fact about the beans and the pests. They can never be reasons which become reasons only when they are conjoined with some particular want. Moral reasons must be reasons independently of what anyone may happen to want: that is why they have to be prescriptive and not informative.

The point was well stated by Wittgenstein in one of his rare excursions into ethical theory:

> Suppose . . . you saw me playing tennis and you said 'Well, you play pretty badly' and suppose I answered 'I know I'm playing badly, but I don't want to play any better', all the other man could say would be 'Ah then, that's all right'. But suppose I had told him a preposterous lie and he came up to me and said 'You're behaving extremely badly', and then I were to say 'I know I behave badly, but then I don't want to behave any better', could he then say 'Ah then, that's all right'? Certainly not; he would say 'Well, you *ought* to want to behave better'. Here you have an absolute judgment of value, where the first instance was one of a relative judgment. The essence of the difference seems to be obviously this: Every judgment of relative value is a mere statement of facts and can therefore be put in such a form that it loses all the appearance of a judgment of value.

Hare's is a formal theory. So far, it does not appear to say anything of what morality is *about*. Isn't this a defect? Don't we want some explanation of why certain kinds of things are wrong – killing, stealing, lying? And certain other things right – charity, loyalty, truthfulness? Surely a set of universal imperatives could be about anything; which is absurd. I shall be dealing with this objection in more detail later – the objection that according to prescriptivism just anything could be right or wrong – but let me deal with it now by once again resorting to the analogy with science. If we compare the universal imperatives of morality with the universal indicatives of science, we see that scientific statements do indeed have to be universal in form: it is not enough to say that this particular piece of copper is expanding, we need something of the form 'all metals expand when heated'. But of course this doesn't mean that *any* universal indicative statement is scientifically acceptable. We aren't allowed to say 'All metals explode when heated'. What, then, are the constraints determining which universal statements are allowed and which are not? Well, to state the obvious, we are not allowed to make universal statements which conflict with what is actually observed. We reject 'All metals explode' simply because here is one that doesn't.

Now, are there similar checks on universal imperatives? There are. We are not allowed to accept the universal imperative 'Kill people whenever you can' because this conflicts with – what? Inhibitions, unreflective convictions, inbuilt restraints, feelings of revulsion? That would do for a start. We need to achieve what John Rawls has called a 'reflective equilibrium'[34] among these various elements and our moral principles, just as we need a similar systematic consistency among experimental observations, hypotheses and high-level theories in science. We can also remind ourselves at this point of the contribution of natural law theory (Chapter VII): only principles the implementation of which do not obviously violate the facts of the human condition will be acceptable as moral guides.

But the most effective check on what universal principles there can be is a feature of the universalisation process itself: what I called (p.55) the second dimension, and what Mackie[35] has called the second stage. When you consider whether you should do X, where X is doing something to another person, you have to consider not just what it would be for anyone to *do* such a thing, but what it would be for anyone to have such a thing *done to them*. And since *you* are just one person among the anyones, this means you have to consider having it done to you. And this, of course, was what the Golden Rule was meant to say (despite Kant's strictures). It has also been called the reversibility test.

Now nobody is willing to be killed, injured, or told lies to, so this second-stage universalisation is indeed a powerful check on moral imperatives. But is it powerful enough? You may object: 'It's not literally true that *nobody* is willing to be killed, or maimed, etc.'; and of course we can identify some exceptions. There are willing partners in suicide pacts. There are people who like being hurt (if there are masochists). And of course there are people who are too stupid or too unimaginative to think out the universalisation process, or too callous to be moved by it. But none of these objections is damaging, because the very same objections could be made, equally worthlessly, against science. Some people are unable to tell red from green; some people are innumerate, or too ham-fisted to perform delicate experiments. This doesn't mean that we can't do science. It just means that we have to reject the minority opinions. In ethics it *may* be the same. It *may* be that we are justified in rejecting the misfits, or at least some of them. No doubt there is a difference of degree here. We can't be as confident, perhaps, in ethics that we have correctly rejected the misfits as we (usually) can in science. But we must postpone further discussion to a later stage.

Before coming to a systematic treatment of the objections to prescriptivism, I need to say something about good and evil, terms which so far have for the most part been overlooked in favour of right and wrong. The relation between the two pairs of key concepts is, as we have seen, a classical problem, and there are labels for types of theory which take one set or the other as primary. Theories which take the good as primary are called teleological, theories which take right and wrong as primary are deontological. Utilitarianism, for instance, is teleological, because it defines right as whatever is productive of the most good (or least evil), good being commonly, though not necessarily, identified with something like happiness. Prescriptivism, as so far described, clearly takes right and wrong as primary, so there is a question where good and bad find a place.

Hare has what almost amounts to a separate theory of good, in terms not of prescribing, but of commending: to call something good is to commend it. However the theory of good and the theory of right can be brought together if we go right back to the starting point, which was that ethics is concerned with answering questions of the form 'What shall I do?'; now we must enlarge this a little, to 'What shall I choose?', where choosing to *do* something, to perform an action, is just one kind of choice. There are at least two other kinds. I can also choose to *have* something, whether a

[125]

book, a television set, a wife, or a goalkeeper. And I can choose to *be* something: a doctor, a dancer, a good citizen. Most of these choices are not, of course, moral choices, just as most decisions to act are not moral decisions. What I call a good book is one which I would choose, or recommend you to choose; a good goalkeeper is one I would select for my team, or recommend you to pick for yours. These choices are not arbitrary (though of course some choices are). They are made for reasons; in the light of standards or criteria. Now we can bring the theory of right and theory of good together under the common heading of criteria. There are criteria for choosing what to do; among these are moral principles, and actions in accordance with them are right. There are criteria for choosing what to have, like cars, thermometers or goalkeepers; none of these are moral criteria, and when we speak of a good car, a good thermometer, or a good goalkeeper, we are not making moral evaluations. And, finally, there are criteria for choosing what to be; even these will mostly not be moral criteria; when we speak of a good doctor or a good dancer, we are not making moral evaluations, but medical or choreographic ones. But *some* of these criteria for choosing what to be will be moral ones; and when we speak of a good man or woman, or of particular sorts of goodness in people, like truthfulness, generosity or courage, or particular sorts of badness, like deceitfulness, cruelty or jealousy, we are making moral evaluations. All that has been said of moral principles, in terms of universality and choice, the objective and the subjective aspects, will apply equally to criteria.

I shall now summarise the respects in which prescriptivism satisfies the conditions for an adequate moral theory. First, the three tests I proposed on p.47. (1) It clearly satisfies the test for an empiricist theory; there is no appeal to the occult or transcendental. (2) It is a mere tautology that it passes the prescriptivity test. (3) It rates at least very highly on the objectivity test. Further, (3a) we have a plausible explanation of why we easily tend to attribute truth and falsity to moral judgments. We left open the question whether moral judgments *are* true or false; but the objectivity conferred by universalisation and the adoption of an impersonal standpoint, and especially the comparison with the corresponding features of science, comes near enough to truth to explain the common vocabulary. At the same time, (4) it also rates highly on what we might call the autonomy test: it gives an account of what it is for the individual moral agent to adopt a morality and to conduct his own moral life.

CHAPTER X

Prescriptivism (4): Objections and replies

I come now to a series of objections to prescriptivism. They can all be met, and showing how they can be resisted will help to strengthen our understanding. The last objection, however, which is the most difficult to meet, does show, I think, that prescriptivism cannot, as hitherto understood, account for quite everything that can count as a morality, though it still accounts for nearly all that is important. These objections are six in number, and fall into two classes, corresponding to the two main and contrasting themes which Hare shares with Kant: individualism, and rationalism. The first set of three objections are to an excess of individualism; the second set of three are objections to an excess of rationalism.

(1) It is frequently objected that we do not *choose* our moral principles. Yet it seems from Hare's account that we do: moral principles are just those universal imperatives that we issue for ourselves and for others; we are not bound either by logic or by the facts of the world to issue one universal imperative rather than another; so it does look as if we *choose* what imperatives to issue, that is, what our moral principles are to be, what we are to 'subscribe to'. And surely, the objection runs, this gives too much freedom to the individual. As one critic has put it, 'such a person is not so much a model as a menace'.[36] Surely (and we may agree)

there must be some control over what principles he adopts. This has already been discussed above; here we may add the following. The answer to this objection is that it assumes, wrongly, that all choices are much of a muchness, whether trivial or serious. Yet it is clear that choosing a career, or choosing a wife, is not like choosing a cigar, or a piece of cake; and neither is choosing a moral principle like these. Just because the word 'choose' is so much at home in trivial contexts like the cigars and cakes, it would certainly be better not to harp on it in moral contexts; but this is not to admit that we are forced to accept our moral principles. We do have a freedom here, though it may be difficult to exercise it. It is useful here, as so often, to compare moral beliefs with factual beliefs. No doubt I *could* choose to believe that the earth is flat, though only at the cost of great effort, involving changing many other beliefs. But when people did believe the earth was flat, it must have been just as difficult to believe that it is round. Yet people were able to believe this, and eventually did. It may be extremely difficult to exercise our intellectual freedom, and to form the belief that the earth is not round. In that sense, I do indeed have little choice. But progress in science has invariably resulted from strong-minded people exercising their intellectual freedom to choose new ways of thinking. Similarly, most of us find it very difficult to adopt any but the conventional moral codes; but those who succeed are the moral pioneers and reformers. They evoke resistance at first, and admiration only later.

So, to conclude, the fact that we all most of the time find ourselves with much the same set of moral principles does not prove that we do not, in some ultimate sense, choose to have them. Everyone, if offered two apples, one sound, one obviously rotten, will take the sound one; that doesn't show that he didn't choose it.

(2) This is a closely related objection. It seems that, according to prescriptivism, anything whatever could be moral or immoral: a position that lends itself to the caricature: there's nothing either right or wrong, but issuing universal imperatives makes it so. Could it be immoral to walk on the lines of the pavement, if some moral thinker came out with this particular prescription? Call that a *weird* morality: is a weird morality possible, or even intelligible?

[129]

Or, to take another extreme case, could there be a morality which is not merely very different from ours, but the exact reverse of it? 'Evil be thou my good,' says Milton's Satan. Call this a diabolical morality. Is such a diabolical morality possible, or even intelligible?

Hare does seem to be committed to saying 'Yes' to both these questions. But is this damaging? Hare defends his position by saying that anyone who adopted such a weird or diabolical morality would be mad; but he claims that there is no reason why insanity should not manifest itself in moral as well as in factual delusions. I am inclined to agree. We cannot prove conclusively that the poor idiot is not the reincarnated Napoleon he claims to be; we cannot even prove conclusively that the flat-earth fanatic is mistaken. Nevertheless are we not entitled to dismiss the views of maniacs and eccentrics in favour of the consensus of well-informed and well-educated people in the community? Just so, why should we not similarly dismiss the moral views of the weirdies or Satans, while acknowledging that they may be sincerely held as moral views? Why should we not dismiss them, likewise, in favour of a consensus of well-intentioned and well-educated persons in the community?

(3) A third objection in terms of excessive individualism or subjectivity involves the concepts of knowledge and belief. (We touched on this topic when discussing intuitionism, p.44). The objector claims that there surely is such a thing as moral knowledge and moral belief. We certainly do say things like 'I know that would be wrong', 'I believe the right thing to do would be . . . '. 'She doesn't know the difference between right and wrong'. Now belief and knowledge strongly imply a propositional content of morality: we know *that* . . ., we believe *that* . . . On the other hand there is no room for believing or knowing in a context of imperatives or prescriptions; so prescriptivism must be inadequate since it gives no account of moral knowledge and belief and indeed seems to make it quite impossible for any such account to be given.

Part of the answer to this has already been given on p.126, where I explained how prescriptivism can accommodate the objective aspects of morality in such a way as to account quite

[130]

naturally for the presence of truth and falsity in our moral vocabulary. The same account will therefore hold for knowledge and belief. But there is more to be said. Of course a full treatment of this topic would require a long excursion into the theory of knowledge which is itself a large department of philosophy. Two points must suffice. One is to point out that knowledge and belief are *not*, as the objector held, excluded in a context of imperatives and prescriptions. The field of law is just such a context, and we have already seen that legal knowledge is fully recognised. The other point is that the proper objects of knowledge and belief are *not*, as the objector held, necessarily propositional. We speak not only of knowing that something is the case, but of knowing how to do things, which will include knowing how to behave; and we speak not only of believing that something is the case, but also of believing *in* something, or in someone. Indeed, the very word 'belief' derives from the notions of trust and faith, which are strongly moral notions.

In one of Saki's short stories, one young man says to another, 'My mother keeps telling me that I ought to know the difference between right and wrong. There is a difference, you know, but I've forgotten what it is.'[37] The absurdity is entertaining, but also illuminating. There must be a difference between two kinds of knowledge, one kind being forgettable and the other not. What distinguishes them? The answer must be that the first kind of knowledge engages mainly at the intellectual level; this is the propositional kind, and it is a matter of assenting to, or dissenting from, propositions, as true or false. The other kind is a matter of assenting to imperatives, and this engages not, principally, with our intellect but with our motivation. This in turn is a matter of *character*, something much more permanent about us than our repertoire of information. Practical knowledge, then, including moral knowledge, will be of this eminently unforgettable kind (though this is not to say that it is totally immune to change or loss).[38] The objection, then, clearly fails.

(4) I conclude that prescriptivism has not over-stated the role of the individual in moral thinking. But I now come to a set of objections from the other side: those that claim that too much has been made of the universal or rational, and too little of the

individual. It will be convenient in some of the discussion to have a pair of labels for the opposed positions. I shall invoke an imaginary opponent called the Existentialist, or E-type: not that I have any particular Existentialist philosopher in mind, but because this is a convenient way of referring to the type of extreme individualist who objects to the Universalist or U-type element in prescriptivism.

An essential feature of any rational attitude, whether theoretical or practical, is (as Hume noted) that it abstracts from a particular concrete situation and classifies one situation with another in respect of this or that common feature. In the Pythagoras example, every triangular object or drawing is in fact different from every other, and so unique; but reason, as exercised by the mathematician, ignores the differences between a triangle of wood and one of perspex, or a triangular diagram drawn in chalk and another drawn in pencil (or even in the mind's eye), and attends instead to a very limited set of common features, the purely geometrical ones. Just so, if there is a rational dimension to morality, the moralist too will have to ignore a great deal of what makes one situation in fact different from another, and attend instead to certain things they have in common, to what he regards as their moral features. If he judges that telling an untruth was wrong, he will attend to the fact that the speaker knew it was untrue, that he intended to deceive, and, perhaps, that he also intended to protect someone from suffering; but he will not attend to the fact that the speaker has blue eyes or is called John. Forming universal imperatives about truth-telling, and applying them, is clearly going to be impossible unless there is a limited selection of relevant features from the unlimited totality of features actually present; if everything has to count, the situation is unique, escapes capture in general terms, and is not universalisable.

Furthermore, as we saw in the discussion of moral progress in Chapter VI, universality is not only an essential feature of morality; it admits of degrees, and it can seem that a more extensive universality, a greater transcending of distinctions, makes for a more 'moral' morality. Just as the science of motion was obstructed by the Aristotelians who clung to the distinction between the terrestrial and the celestial, so the development of a truly human morality required the transcending of the distinctions between bond and free, man and woman, white and coloured.

Yet this tendency to abstract still further from the particularities of human relationships has its dangers. Plato represents Euthyphro as preening himself on his 'advanced morality'[39] when he does precisely this, in proposing to take legal action against his own father just as he would against a stranger. Plato plainly disapproves, and so should we: what has been obliterated here is itself a *moral* distinction. It appears that an essential feature of morality, after all, is a certain sensitivity to a particular human predicament; something other than the universal just is what counts. Our Existentialist will claim, accordingly, that any judgment which fails to reckon with the unique situation, in all its concrete totality, as a U-type judgment must, is a defective moral judgment, a case of 'bad faith'.

Let us begin to deal with this by placing the U-type versus E-type issue in a wider setting. Let us assume, uncontroversially, that both U-type and E-type evaluations do have a place somewhere in human life, not necessarily, of course, in the same place. By 'evaluations' here I mean to include judgments, verdicts, criticisms of any kind, scientific, moral, aesthetic, or any other kind there may be; and, of course, both favourable and unfavourable evaluations. Examples will be: of course, moral judgments; but also, expressions of admiration or contempt of non-moral kinds; expressions of loyalty to a particular person or institution (which may conflict with moral evaluations); and expressions of affection and dislike, friendship or animosity, between persons. We may also look at these evaluations from the point of view of the persons or things evaluated, and speak of the claims they make on us.

The distinction between U-type and E-type evaluations is most easily formulated in terms of logic: E-type evaluations necessarily contain proper names or some other singular mode of reference, while U-type evaluations necessarily contain only predicates. In other words, E-type evaluations mention particular individuals, while U-type evaluations either do not mention individuals at all,

[133]

or mention them only as bearers of properties. For example, an expression of affection, someone speaking of his beloved, is E-type because it has to mention, or contextually imply, a particular beloved person; if someone says he is in love, and is asked 'With which girl'? – it will be unintelligible if he says 'With no particular girl'; whereas, to take a U-type 'love', if he says he loves strawberries, the opposite case is the unintelligible one: it makes no sense to ask which particular strawberry, or berries, he loves.[40] Similarly with at least some aesthetic evaluations; we have to know whether the critic is talking about *La Gioconda*, the *Moonlight Sonata*, or some other unique object; and with expressions of loyalty, some particular leader or institution must be mentioned, such as Mrs Thatcher, New Zealand, or the NUM. (But not quite always, as we shall see.)

The question now is: are moral evaluations U-type or E-type? According to Kant and his followers, moral evaluations are necessarily U-type; they cannot contain proper names, except incidentally. According to the Existentialist, they are essentially E-type. And a third possible position is that they could be either or both. Hare is committed to the Kantian position, that they are always U-type. He defends this view against critics in an article from which I quote an extract in the form of a dialogue in which 'K' (for Kantian) corresponds to my 'U':

E. You oughtn't to do that.

K. So you think one oughtn't to do that kind of thing?

E. I think nothing of the sort: I say only that *you* oughtn't to do *that*.

K. Don't you even imply that a person like me in circumstances of this kind oughtn't to do that kind of thing when the other people involved are the sort of people that they are?

E. No; I only say that *you* oughtn't to do *that*.

K. Are you making a moral judgment?

E. Yes.

K. In that case I fail to understand your use of the word 'moral'.[41]

We are expected to share K's bafflement. Here is the strongest possible thesis that moral judgments are necessarily U-type, and that this is so in virtue of the very meaning of the word 'moral'.

[134]

But is it?

We have seen that, outside morals at least, there are E-type judgments, and judgments that are intermediate: they can contain either type or both. Aesthetic judgments very often contain descriptions of *features* of works of art, which are U-type, even though they also refer, indispensably, to particular works as well. Coming nearer to morality, we seem to have an intermediate type in the case of loyalty: this is E-type in so far as loyalty to a particular leader or institution is involved, but at the same time it is also U-type in so far as there is a necessary presumption that *anything* that the leader requires is to be done, and not just by me but by all loyalists. Even closer to morality, and arguably right inside it, is the case of patriotism – loyalty to a country. (This is why I entered a *caveat* about loyalty.) Patriotism, it seems, comes in two forms, one pure U-type, the other mixed. Patriotism is a matter of pure U-type evaluation if one approves of people showing loyalty to their country whichever country it is; but it is a mixed type, if one approves only of people showing loyalty to a particular country, usually the country of the speaker. It is an interesting fact of social psychology that E-type patriotism is more evident in times of war. It is only in peace-time that one can easily admire the patriotic exploits of former enemies. Now if moral evaluations were fully universalisable, and this were a defining characteristic of the word 'moral', as the quotation from Hare asserts, then one brand of patriotism could be moral, but the other not.

Can thoroughgoing universalism be challenged? A fairly typical criticism from the 'Existentialist' point of view goes like this. Deducing a moral decision or verdict from a moral rule is often not possible and often not desirable. Morality cannot, and should not, legislate for all cases. Anyone who thinks it can and should is a mere casuist, someone corrupted by the legal model, who thinks of moral conduct as simply conformity to fixed rules, and leaves no room for the necessary spontaneity of moral choice.

Something is obviously amiss here, because we have seen that both Kant and Hare go out of their way to emphasise the importance of the moral freedom of the individual. There are at least two mistakes in the critic's objection. He is mistaken in thinking that universalism implies that duties are deducible from general rules; or, even if they are, that such rules would have to be abstract general rules (like 'lying is wrong'). Let us take this second point first. The very word 'rule' (and the word 'principle') can be misleading, because it does suggest something that is statable, and statable briefly, in a simple formula. But what is involved in a moral decision can, of course, be extremely complex. Moral principles – or, better perhaps, acting and thinking on principle in moral contexts – can take account of any amount of complexity of detail in actual real life situations. A person who acts on principle does not necessarily act on a *simple* principle. (In Hare's imaginary conversation, the reply of 'K', 'So you think . . .', makes this clear.)

Even so, the Existentialist might still have a case on the first point. Does not universalism indeed imply that duties and decisions about particular cases are deducible from rules, even if the rules are not necessarily simple? And isn't this putting the cart before the horse? Surely, the E-type man may say, particular moral judgments are not derived from general moral principles; rather, particular moral judgments come first, and moral principles only come later, if at all, as formal codifications of actual judgments, or as short-hand rules for making more judgments. This suggests a sort of Inductive Theory of moral principles. An actual example of this Inductive Theory is Rule-Utilitarianism: moral principles are guides to discovering what sort of action is likely to be maximally productive of happiness, just as empirical generalisations (in the ordinary, science-related inductive theory) are guides to discovering what sorts of event are likely to happen after other sorts of event.

Now the Existentialist is right in his premises, but wrong in his conclusions. He is right to say that moral judgments are not, or not always, derived from general principles. There isn't a general principle which has to precede every moral judgment. But he is wrong to conclude that generalisation has no place at all, or that it comes only later and incidentally. What sort of involvement is this, if not deductive? Well, a single moral judgment does imply, presuppose, or (best of all) commit the speaker to, a general judgment, in the very act of judging. If no such generalisation is involved, it is indeed difficult to see how moral judgment is going on. Compare again the case of the geometrical theorem. This is certainly not deduced from a general principle that what is true of this triangle is true of all triangles: it is deduced from axioms or other theorems. Yet my asserting this theorem, even if it is a brand-new one, does commit me to asserting it on all other occasions, and expecting others to agree with me about it. Unless I am committed in this way, what I am doing is not geometry. (Of course, the Existentialist will not accept the analogy with geometry, but that is not the point.)

What about the inductive theory? We can agree that there is a superficial analogy here. There is in ethics something analogous to rejecting a hypothesis in the face of a counter-instance (that all swans are white, in face of the black swan). As a doctor, say, I may reject my life-long principle against euthanasia, when I eventually encounter a case where it strikes me as obviously the right thing to do. But these cases are really very different. If I do reject a moral principle because I come across a situation where it would yield the verdict 'wrong' and I want to insist that in fact the verdict should be 'right', what happens is that in making the new moral judgment I thereby set up for myself a new moral principle which contradicts the old one and supersedes it. But to take the Inductive Theory seriously would imply that we go through a process of collecting specimens of conduct, identify them with labels, discover to our interest that all the collected specimens turn out to be further characterisable as right (or wrong), and so finally risk a generalisation that all future specimens will turn out to be similarly right (or wrong). This is plainly a caricature of moral thinking. In the case of the swans, there are independent ways of finding out that a creature is a swan, and that it is white (or black); but in the case of euthanasia, there are *not* independent ways of finding out that this is a case of releasing someone with his consent from incurable pain, and that this is right (or wrong) *as well*. There is no 'as well' about it. This point is well made by Hare in another context where he is talking about another value word, 'good'. He points out that it is perfectly all right to say, of two motor cars, that this one is exactly similar to that one, except that this one is red and the other isn't; but that it is unintelligible to say that this car is exactly like that one, except that this one is good and the other isn't. In my example, this swan can be exactly like that one, except that it is black; but this case of euthanasia cannot be exactly like that one, except that it is right. It can only be right *because of* some general feature it has which the other lacks.

Continuing this defence of universalism, then – that what is universal in morality is not something from which judgments or decisions are derivable, and so it is no objection to point out that they are not – we can put it another way, in terms of the contrast between *form* and *content*. An imperative expression requires some action in virtue of its content: what it actually says. It can be either E-type of U-type or both; examples of all three would be: 'Give this to Cynthia'; 'Be kind to Cynthia'; 'Keep your promises'. Now the Universalisation Principle, or what we might call the Reformed Categorical Imperative, does not require *any* action, not even of the most general kind. If it did, it would have to be something like 'Be good', or 'Do what is right', which are empty tautologies: the ethical counterparts, in fact, of the factual tautology 'What is the case is the case'. What the Categorical Imperative does require is the *form* of the particular moral imperative: it requires that it be U-type, not E-type. But the 'should' here is logical, not moral.

We might also speak of a rule of procedure, as opposed to a rule of substance. If you break a rule of substance, you commit an offence; but if you break a rule of procedure, you are not playing the game. There is a difference between breaking the offside rule in football, and riding up and down the pitch on horseback. There are plenty of offences to be committed when playing the moral game; but to be playing the game at all you must be following the rule 'Always universalise'. Now it would be absurd to suggest that one might get positive moral guidance from a rule of procedure, just as it would be to seek guidance from the 'rule': 'Always sleep on it before taking a serious decision'. Again we have the theoretical parallel: in looking for the cause of iron rusting, we work with a Principle of Uniformity of Nature; but it is no use trying to find the cause of rusting *from* the principle.

But perhaps the Existentialist still has a case against an *excess* of formality. There is nothing wrong with basing your moral judgment on the features of the situation, but there *is* something wrong with basing your judgment on an *inadequate review* of the features, or on a set of features picked out by some *conventional code*. This is the grain of truth in the Existentialist's complaint about 'bad faith' or 'inauthenticity'. And there is also a grain of truth in his emphasis on the 'unutterable particularity' of real life situations. This is not an objection to universalist theory, but it may well be a sound objection to a certain style of U-type writing. There has always been a temptation, whether because of lack of space or, more likely, lack of imagination, to discuss problems of ethical theory in terms of a few over-simplified and stereotyped examples, like unposted letters and borrowed books. Existentialism is certainly a valuable reminder that this is not the stuff of the moral life. A single moral situation may well be so complex that it takes an entire novel to state it (and perhaps another novel to resolve it). Novels, in fact (and I do not mean philosophical novels like those of J.P. Sartre) are very important for moral philosophy. In the present context we may note: a novel typically presents a morally problematic situation; it does so by presenting all and (preferably) only those features which are morally relevant; the situation is, of course, unique (since every novel is different), yet it is presented entirely in terms of general features; even the characters, who would be particular individuals if they were real, are, since they are fictional, nothing more than the bearers of properties, stated or implied. Here we have an illustration of the interplay of the universal and the particular in the moral life.

To summarise this long discussion of the first objection to the universalist theme in prescriptivism, I shall make a couple of points about the link with the basic idea of prescriptivity.

First, it is essential to morality that it should be action-guiding for ordinary people; and this entails that, like any other set of public rules or standards (thought no doubt more complex and more flexible), it must enable people to recognise the moral relevance of certain features of their situations. In other words, moral distinctions cannot be such that only moral experts can detect them. Secondly, and much the same point, morality must be *teachable*. When I referred to Plato's question about this, on p.1

[139]

of the Introduction, I said that morality, though not taught in courses of formal instruction, is nevertheless taught: by such methods as precept and example. But a precept has to be *understood*: and this means being able to recognise the *kind* of situations to which it applies; and to see something or someone as an *example*, one needs to recognise what *sort* of things it, he or she is an example *of*. (This is not to say, of course, that one must be able to produce a verbal formula.) Now a thoroughly E-type morality is, presumably, not teachable. This may not worry the Existentialist, who will dismiss the teachable part of morality as convention, and deference to it as bad faith. But this, as I said before, is a confusion: between a limited set of simple rules, which is admittedly inadequate, and a refined and developing moral awareness which is still essentially universalising. Moral sensitivity and discrimination are certainly all-important, but even – indeed especially – they are not acquired without training and practice.

(5) A fifth objection can be dismissed more briefly. This is the problem of the insincere universaliser. The objection is that universality is too wide to capture the essence of morality, because it covers both sincere and insincere, genuine and bogus moral attitudes. There is such a thing as special pleading. Suppose someone wants people to think he is making a moral judgment when in fact he is only expressing a prejudice or personal interest. He can always *say* that he is making a universalisable judgment – he would be prepared to say the same about anyone else in similar circumstances; especially if he can afford to assume that similar circumstances are very unlikely to recur. He can even take steps to ensure that they will not recur, by making his statement of the relevant circumstances sufficiently specific. To take an absurd example, I might say 'I think I ought to be paid £50,000 a year; of course I think any other philosophy teacher ought to be paid the same, provided that he is blue-eyed, six feet tall, and works in a building by the sea'. This example is absurd only because it is utterly ingenuous. There are plenty of actual claims, including wage claims, which are not too far removed from this.

This objection, however, is not only without force: it can be turned on its head in defence of universalism. Insincerity is a special case of deceit or falsity: being false about one's own intentions. (We may allow cases of self-deception, too.) Now not all statements can be false; lies are only possible if most statements are true, so that there is a standing presumption of truth in utterances. So, insincerity about one's own intentions is only possible if most expressions of intent are sincere. Not all, or even most, such expressions can be insincere. And in the present case, if there is such a thing as moral insincerity, there must be genuine cases of moral attitudes which the insincere ones are pretending to be: and their pretence will only work, and can only be attempted, if the pretended universalisability really is a feature of genuine morality. Hypocrisy, it has been said, is the homage that vice pays to virtue. Just so, special pleading is the homage that inclination and self-interest[42] pay to morality. In the case of hypocrisy about virtue, people who are really wicked pretend virtue; and in the case of special pleading, people who are really motivated by inclination or self-interest pretend to be motivated by moral considerations, which have to be seen to be universalisable. In both cases the pretence is possible only if there actually is something that is both real, and worth pretending to be: namely, virtue, and a universal moral viewpoint.

(6) This objection is much the most serious and fundamental one. It has a good deal in common with the 'Existentialist' but avoids his mistakes; and it is the only one which cannot be answered without making certain adjustments to universalism. It goes like this: universalisability is not a necessary condition of morality, but only of *rational* morality; and then only in so far as morality is a matter of moral reasons. For universalisability attaches only to reasons, in so far as they are reasons, but this has nothing to do with morality as such. And morality, according to the objection, is not (only) a matter of reasons: there are other dimensions to morality than that of rationality, even if we add the autonomy thesis about the individual's role in freely choosing and taking responsibility for his (rational) decisions.

Now I have to agree that the universalists have indeed taken a strongly rationalistic line about morality; and that this can indeed be brought into question. Suppose we start with a re-statement of the individual (as opposed to social) aspect of morality.[43] From the point of view of myself as agent, my morality consists, not in what other people insist that I should do, but in what *I* insist that I should do. So far, this is only a re-statement of the autonomy thesis. But suppose we go on to claim, against Kant, that morality does not necessarily involve the idea of general rules and principles; that it is both logically and psychologically possible for me to think that I am morally obliged to do something wihout thinking that anybody else in a similar situation is or would be obliged to do it. There are cases where an individual finds himself subject to a call, a mission, which imposes on him distinct obligations without general import. Biblical prophets say things like 'The word of the Lord came unto me, saying . . . '. In a Western film, a John Wayne-type character says something like 'A guy's gotta do what he's gotta do' – and this is not a tautology.

It looks, then, as if classical prescriptivism falls short because, in spite of its emphasis on the autonomy of the individual, it *is* too firmly wedded to generalities. It is not enough to picture the individual as choosing, adopting, his own general rules; he does not have to go by general rules at all; there may be, as we have seen, individual obligations without general import. Perhaps what is needed to supplement prescriptivism is a closer attention to the psychological aspect of morality, as opposed to the social one. The social aspect of morality certainly does involve general rules and patterns of behaviour; without these, as I have said, morality could not be taught, transmitted, or even discussed. But what morality is like from the inside, though overlapping with the external aspect, can also depart from it. What I insist on for myself need not be exactly what I insist on for other people, nor what they insist on for me, nor what I expect them to insist on. I may expect others to share my rules of daily conduct, but not my aspirations. There are moral situations, even if they are rare, in which the prophet, saint, hero, or even the ordinary man, *finds himself* under the sway of a categorical imperative which is for him alone. He tends to say 'I must', 'I can't', 'I just feel it wouldn't be right'. And these need not be (though of course they may be) symptoms of mere inarticulacy.

We must not allow this line of thought to go too far. I can agree that, if I am thinking of what is right or wrong for me, one of these

E-type expressions could be a genuine moral judgment. But contrast this with the case where I make a judgment about somebody else. Could I still, in the third-personal case, go on saying things like 'I feel it wouldn't be right', 'You just can't'? Could I ever say to someone that *he* ought to act in such a way, even though I could give no reasons, and am not even prepared to say that if I or anyone else were in his situation I or they ought to act in the same way? I think not, and that Hare was quite right to call this unintelligible. (Connected with this is the fact that we can say that my conscience tells me what I should do, but we cannot say that it tells me what you or she should do.) A crucial difference, however, remains: between commenting on other people's conduct, which does commit me to generality, and thinking about my own, which sometimes, apparently, does not. We seem, moreover, to have a place here for that positive aspect of morality which I discussed in Chapter V as standing in sharp contrast with the legal model. The morality of the saint, hero, or aspirant presses against the bounds of rationality, yet without ceasing thereby to be a morality.

To deal adequately with this demand, we must undertake a review of different types or styles of moral thinking and its associated vocabulary. So far we have been concerned mainly with one style, which takes as its paradigm judgments of right and wrong. We have looked from time to time at a different, but related, style, which has good and evil as its key terms. We must now find room for a third. Let me set out these three styles, distinguishing them systematically in several respects: first, in terms of typical specimens, both of primary judgments and of associated ethical theories; next, their implicit models; their key terms; their characteristic types of motivation; their possible natural basis or origin; and, finally, how they stand with respect to the universalisability feature.

A *The ethics of obligation.* This style is exemplified by the Decalogue; its chief theoretical exponent is Kant. Its model is, of course, the law. Its key terms are: action, what (not) to do; duty, principle, rule; sin, crime; ought, right, wrong. Its motivational factors comprise sanctions, censure, remorse, self-respect, and generally a minimum standard below which one must not fall. Its natural basis is human survival, or the minimum conditions of tolerable social existence. Its judgments are fully universalisable.

B *The ethics of emulation*. This style is exemplified by the Sermon on the Mount, or (a very different sub-style) the Homeric maxim 'Always excel'; its model is education (in the sense of character-formation, being well brought up); its chief theorist is Aristotle; its key terms are: states of character, what sort of person to be; ideals, standards, virtue, vice. The motivations are more positive: incentives, ambition, a maximum standard to be approached, praise, admiration. Its natural basis will be not just staying alive, but a certain quality of life in a community. It too is universalisable, though not unquestionably so, since not all virtues are fully compatible. The universalisation of justice may exclude that of mercy. (We shall review this question shortly.)

C *The ethics of aspiration*. This style is exemplified by the saint, hero, prophet, martyr, and by the award of honours for distinguished conduct. It has no theoretical examples, or models. Its key terms will be, apart from aspiration itself: mission, calling, and the technical term 'act of supererogation'. Its motivation will not be easily categorised. Its natural basis will not be evident. And it is, according to the original argument, non-U.

Acts of supererogation are defined as going beyond the call of duty. But it is important to distinguish these cases from certain cases which *are* cases of (mere) duty, but where doing one's duty is exceptionally difficult. The ship's captain who is last to abandon ship, perhaps losing his life, has not performed an act of supererogation, but an act of duty in difficult circumstances. (We can see this if we try to imagine him shouldering aside the women and children in a frantic dash for the lifeboat.) Or take an even harder case: the Cologne maniac.[44] A woman is teaching in a single-class village school when an escaped madman armed with a flame-thrower appears at the window and opens fire. The teacher rushes outside to confront the maniac, who turns, and incinerates her. This macabre example reminds us that even a teacher's ordinary duty of care may in an extreme case require the ultimate sacrifice. (Readers may exercise their casuistical powers to avoid this conclusion.) Both captain and teacher are to be praised and admired to the uttermost, but only because doing your duty in such peculiar and arduous circumstances requires not only respect for duty (type A morality) but also courage and determination of a high order (type B). For a genuine example of supererogation, we can take a fairly stock example: that of the soldier who throws himself on an accidentally dropped live grenade to save his comrades. This is supererogatory as defined; the hero might well have thought 'Someone has to do it', but since duties cannot attach to *someone* (but to no one in particular), it was no one's duty, and so not his. Yet we may suppose him to have thought *he* had to do it, even though no one else had to – an explicit case of an E-type obligation.

However, we still are not forced to conclude that the universalisability feature must be abandoned, not even in the extreme case of type C ethics. True, what I aspire to, what I take as my mission, what I uniquely have to do – are not to be extended to others, even if they are in all other respects like myself. Not, that is, as obligations to *do* as I do. But there are two respects in which universality remains. First, only the second stage of universalisation is affected – the extension from myself to others, or *vice versa*. The first stage remains in force. Whatever I take my mission to be, it is a continuing mission; I am indefinitely committed to it; if it is a recent one, I will tend to regret the part of my life when I lacked it (like St Paul, perhaps, after his conversion). Even the grenade hero could have thought, if he had time, that he would have done the same thing on another such occasion.

But universality also remains even at the second stage. What has been broken, or loosened, is a certain link between thought and action. But the universality remains at the level of thought. I cannot demand that others perform acts of supererogation; but I admire them when they do. I cannot expect others to engage in my missions; but I am, at the very least, likely to approve if they do, or if they engage in other missions. (Of course I may also disapprove, but this will be no different from disapproving of those who adopt conflicting principles – type A.) We can see now that the same applies to the morality of emulation (type B). There was a question about universalisability where virtues are not fully compatible. But being just, and being charitable, are each admirable in a fully universalisable way; the difference is that, here too, the link between such judgments and action is less direct. One may have to choose acts, or policies of action, which are both just and less than charitable. Yet even the choice may be rationally appraisable.

I conclude that, with suitable qualifications, prescriptivism can accommodate the difficult cases of extreme agent-centred moralities. The modifications, I believe, far from weakening the theory, make for an enrichment.

CHAPTER XI

Form and content

These terms represent the horns of a dilemma that tends to beset
any attempts to deal with what I have called the central question
of ethical theory: how to find a definition of 'moral'. What
distinguishes moral judgments, decisions, considerations, from
non-moral ones? Is it that moral considerations just *are* things like
killing and stealing? That would lead to a definition in terms of
content. Or are moral considerations a matter of what we choose
to prescribe universally? That will yield a definition in terms of
form. If we take the first alternative, defining morality in terms of
a necessary content ('Right means telling the truth and keeping
promises')[45] we come up against the objections to naturalism,
such as the lack of prescriptivity or action-guiding force, the
is-ought gap. If, on the other hand, we adopt a formal definition,
we can write in these features: we can say that moral judgments
are those made in accordance with action-guiding principles; but
we then get another sort of objection, because it seems to follow
that morality has no essential content of its own; anything could
be moral or immoral, since there are no formal limits to what an
eccentric or diabolical moralist might choose to take as principles
for guiding his, and other people's, lives. We have already met
this point at least twice before. As an objection to prescriptivism
(the second objection) I dealt with it by agreeing with Hare that
there can be ethical as well as factual delusions. But I now have to

admit that that was only a stop-gap answer; and that more needs to be said.

We can only distinguish the sane from the insane if there is an *objective* basis for the distinction. What is the objectivity in ethics that controls and limits an individual's choice of morality? What corresponds here to the objectivity of science, history, and so on, which controls and limits the beliefs of the scientist and the historian, and enables us in these other fields to reject with confidence the crank, the eccentric and the madman? Is a consensus of like-minded people really enough? This is where I left the discussion at p.123, where I undertook to resume it here. Notice that we are still facing much the same dilemma: how to accommodate in one ethical theory two obvious and apparently irreconcilable facts: autonomy, or the freedom of the individual in some sense to choose his morality, and objectivity, which restricts and perhaps even cancels that very freedom.

Let us take up directly, then, the issue of formalism. Critics have complained that formal theories (such as prescriptivism) leave the content of morality wholly unspecified; the critics, on the contrary, think the content of morality is quite specific. What determines this content, and makes it objective, is just one big fact about morality: the fact that it is, in some deep sense, *useful*, profitable, advantageous, beneficial. The critics differ over the question 'beneficial to whom?'; some take a more egoistic line, that it must pay the individual to be good; others, that it must pay someone, most people, but not necessarily everyone. I prefer to leave to the last chapter the question 'Does it pay *me* to be moral?', since this seems to belong naturally to the end of things. I shall take first the more general line, that it must pay *someone*. A typical expression of this view is this:

> My own view is that morality has some at least roughly specificable content . . . It appears at least enormously plausible to say that one who professes to be making a moral judgment *must* at least profess that what is at issue is the good or harm, well-being or otherwise, of human beings – that what he regards as morally wrong is somehow damaging, and what he regards as morally right is somehow beneficial.[46]

[148]

There are echoes here of natural law theory, which I criticised at the time not as false but as inadequate; it covered only what is referred to here as harm and damage, and perhaps only a part of that: it was concerned only with the minimal conditions of survival for a society. Certainly this very negative account has to be supplemented with something positive. But has the writer supplied one? He frankly admits, in the same passage, a 'high degree of vagueness' and that the view contains 'a hornet's nest of problems'.

The hornet's nest might well be this. Take the list of terms on which so much depends, centering on the key concepts of benefit and harm. We have, alongside benefit: profit, gain, satisfaction (of need or interest), fulfilment, welfare, well-being, happiness. Alongside harm we have the corresponding negative terms, evil, loss, damage, injury, unsatisfied need, lack of fulfilment, being in a bad way, unhappiness. Now a difficulty arises about all or most of these terms. There is a certain double meaning: the duality of fact and value. When we say that something is beneficial or damaging, profitable or injurious, *are* we stating a fact about it, or are we making an evaluation which can be challenged? Suppose a starving man says 'I need some food', and a rich company director says 'I need a Rolls Royce'. Everyone will agree that the starving man needs food and that he ought to get some. But not everyone would agree that the rich man ought to get a Rolls. Again, take happiness. We would not call a person happy just because he happens to have certain desires and they have been satisfied, but only if they are desires *of the right sort*, only if we don't disapprove of his evil or perverted desires, or of his unscrupulous ways of satisfying them. (Compare congratulations: we can't congratulate someone on a successful fraud or robbery.) So an ethical theory based on terms like benefit, harm, happiness, is viciously circular, because it claims to show why morality must concern itself with certain things, but it only shows that morality concerns itself with what we think we *ought* to concern ourselves with.

However, I do want to agree that the theory in question is basically sound, and can survive the criticisms. I do want to say that it is just true that a starving man needs food, and it is just false that anyone ever needs a Rolls-Royce; it is just an abuse of language to say so. I am also inclined to agree with Plato that the evil tyrant just is not happy, and that this is not merely an expression of my personal evaluation of his perverted desires and cruel means of satisfaction. Can we justify the inclination to say these things?

Unfortunately the terms benefit, welfare, happiness are the most difficult ones; let us start at an easier point and work up to them. Take first 'injury' and its associated concept 'dangerous'. These are clear and objective enough: we have no choice but to regard bulls, say, as rather dangerous, and if someone has lost his hand in an accident we have no choice but to say that he has been injured. The is-ought gap seems to have disappeared. To clinch the matter, let us go even further back, outside the human person (but not the human context). Take the case of damage to a bicycle, car or other artefact. Here the evaluation is so closely tied to the description that a broken bicycle (beyond a certain point) cannot even be called a bicycle, but perhaps a heap of scrap that was once a bicycle. A table with a missing leg is no longer a table.

What this shows is that very many ordinary things have the concept of a *function* built into them: the very meaning of the word for the thing includes a reference to what the thing is *for*. Such words then are not purely descriptive, if this means descriptive of actual features. It is part of the meaning of 'table' that a table does have a flat horizontal surface, supported at a certain height; but it is also part of the meaning (and the more important part) that a table is *for* putting things on, eating off, and so on, and anything that cannot serve these purposes is necessarily and objectively either not a table at all, or a bad table.

To bring this out, suppose that, in the grip of an extreme version of the autonomy thesis, we were to try separating the evaluative from the descriptive aspects of the term 'damage'. We should get: (1) X is changed from state S1 to S2; this is descriptive and objective; and (2) X ought not to be changed to S2; this is evaluative and, perhaps, subject to the individual's choice.

But *do* we have autonomy with respect to (2)? Surely at the very least our autonomy is very strictly curtailed. We cannot (logically cannot) be indifferent about, or adopt positively different values, ends, or purposes *and still mean the same* by the word 'table'. Understanding here strictly controls evaluation.

The only autonomy we do have is remote and rare, but worth noting. We are, ultimately, free to take part in, or alternatively, to opt out of, a certain way of life: the way of life which alone gives a meaning to words like 'table', because it includes a recognised use for such things *and* their words, while another way of life (the traditional Japanese, in the case of tables) does not.[47]

It might be objected that tables and bicycles are trivial and unhelpful examples. Certainly they are things of minor importance; but their connection with moral affairs is not slender. The point is that they are not merely objects, but artificial objects. Artefacts were important enough even for Plato to be constantly referring to examples like knives, spindles and pruning-hooks. (This could seem remarkable for two reasons: in a non-technological age, one might have thought there would be too few artefacts to make an impact on philosophical thinking; one might add (borrowing a line from Oscar Wilde) that the aristocratic Plato had probably never *seen* a pruning-hook.) What is important about artefacts is that they are the very things closest to man, being made by him for his purposes, and so are more likely than anything else to reflect something about his values.

From damaged artefacts we pass to injured limbs. Here it may seem to be an important difference that human limbs and organs are not, like artefacts, made by man (artificial limbs and organs, or course, excluded) and so it seems that they cannot have the concept of a function built into them, as artefacts have, because they were not made *for* a function (unless they were so made by a god; but the *meaning* of words like 'hand' or 'liver' cannot depend on theological beliefs). However, I think it would be a mistake to suppose that the concept of function is not built into terms like heart, liver, eye, even though those things were not made *for* a function. We can see this if we ask what is the standard procedure for identifying particular organs or limbs, especially if it is of an unfamiliar organism. We do not just inspect *appearances* for something that *looks like* an eye or liver, but by finding out how it is used, what its function is.[48]

So far, we have had only non-moral evaluations. To come

closer to moral values, we shall have to consider whether the functional vocabulary can be extended to human beings themselves, as Plato argued it could. And here we do get into some difficulty, because everyday language is not of much help. In the case of artefacts and organs, it was; but we are now speaking of whole beings, not instruments or working parts of some larger whole. But it is worth noting that, when human beings *are* instruments or organs of some larger whole, as they can be, then evaluation in terms of function becomes immediately intelligible. We speak perfectly easily of a good bricklayer, a bad driver, a good sergeant or general. Here again the evaluations are strictly related to function. It was said of the late Pablo Picasso that he was a good painter but a bad father.[49] Without function-relativity, this would be a contradiction. If something is a red cube, it is red; and if something is a green block, it is green; so the same thing can't be both a red cube and a green block, because it would have to be both red and green, which is a contradiction.[50] But it does *not* follow that if someone is a good painter, he is good, or that, if he is a bad father, he is bad; no contradiction arises if someone is said to be both, just because good and bad are function-dependent, the functions in question being themselves quite compatible: painting and paternity.

In these cases, then, we can arrive immediately at value-judgments, just as we could with tables and limbs. Any act which consisted in depriving a bricklayer of his ability to lay bricks would be automatically a bad act in virtue of the very meaning of the word 'bricklayer'. (Of course this doesn't mean that such an act would necessarily be morally evil: it might be a surgical operation necessary for his health.) And from the point of view of bricklaying, or generalship, or whatever, we again have no choice but to evaluate these things in one way. The only autonomy here is again the remote one of opting out of the way of life, of rejecting the point of view, that alone gives meaning to bricklaying or generalship. (Perhaps the latter option is not so remote, for the pacifist.)

But what about the central case of *moral* good and evil? Is there something which, as human beings, we cannot opt out of? Life itself? Or a characteristically human sort of life, whatever that means? Something like this will be needed if we are to find the objective, necessary basis for morality.

Do human beings as such have a function? Most people would resist this, saying that this is an illegitimate extension from the field of artefacts and other things that do have functions; or that it leads to, or stems from, unplausible metaphysical assumptions about man as a creature designed by a supernatural inventor, or evolved by occult cosmic purposes.

However, I think we can give some sense to the idea of a function of man, thereby agreeing with Plato, and still more with Aristotle, yet without such dubious metaphysical assumptions. I shall start with another example from the sub-human field: not an artefact or organ, but an organism. Take Hume's example of the oak tree. A tree is a biological object. And biological objects like trees are not either instruments or organs (not, that is, as themselves; they can of course be *put* to use, but this is true even of human beings, as we have seen.) Now we are perfectly familiar with the kind of evaluation expressed by speaking of perfect specimens, or alternatively of poor or fair ones. Moreover our judgments agree in a way we should expect if they are based on something objective. We should think someone eccentric, incomprehensible or insane, if he went out of his way to seek out and admiringly contemplate stunted, distorted, starved or mutilated oak trees, and despised as worthless what the rest of us would call fine specimens. Would not the destruction of such a fine specimen be a bad act? If we hesitate to say so, this is only because we may doubt whether it would be *morally* bad, but that is not the point (though I would indeed be tempted to think that the deliberate destruction of a fine tree for no reason whatever, just for fun, *would* be a morally bad act, like killing animals for sport). Why would it be bad? We do not have an obvious functional dependence here, as we did in the case of the act that was bad for someone's bricklaying. But we do have something. We do have a fairly clear idea of the *potentialities* of things: potentialities which can be either developed and realised, or stunted and thwarted; we have the idea of flourishing as opposed to languishing.

Can we apply this to human beings? We will need to ask, what are the potentialities which are specifically human, such that

[153]

stunting and thwarting them will be necessarily bad. Plato came up with two suggestions in the *Republic*[51]: one was 'deliberating, commanding, controlling', and the other, 'living'. Each of these is inadequate; the first mostly reflects merely the virtues and skills of the ruling classes, while the second includes the animal and the vegetable. But if we join the two together and expand a bit, we get something more plausible. Control and life together imply, and certainly implied for Plato, the activity of directing one's own life, as well as, possibly, that of others, by something for which the Greeks conveniently had one word: *logos*, which means both speech and reason. This element certainly distinguishes human from sub-human life.[52] It also goes with many other things which seem to be specifically human attributes, such as foresight, calculation, and planning, and also much that is at first sight non-rational or emotional but still specifically human, such as memory, hope, concern for the future, and for the absent. All these potentialities for a full human life can be either frustrated or developed, which will be bad and good respectively.

But are they *necessarily* bad and good? This will depend on whether these potentialities are just a set of facts we happen to know about human beings, or whether they are part of the very meaning of what it is to be human. And there can be little doubt of the answer. Going back to the table: we saw that the 'potentialities' of the table – what tables are for – enters directly into the meaning of the word. Can we say that *what man is for* enters into the very meaning of the word *man*? Suppose it doesn't: suppose we try to say, again in the grip of an extreme autonomy thesis, that man is not 'for' anything, and that each of us is free to decide for himself or herself what he or she is 'for', what to make of one's life: so that this does *not* enter into the meaning of the word for what we are. But this will not work. It is true that *what man is for* is not explicitly built-in to the meaning of 'man' in the way in which bricklaying is explicitly built-in to the word 'bricklayer'. But something is built-in. Consider first the word 'man' in its narrower sense. (It is, of course, notorious (and inconvenient) that the English language is peculiar in not having a word for 'man' meaning 'human being', but only a word for 'male human being' which has to do duty for female human beings as well.) In its

[154]

narrow sense, then, we say things like 'Be a man', 'Don't be unmanly', 'He's a real man', or (more explicitly) 'He's a real he-man' – referring to certain qualities which male human beings are expected to possess. Similarly for female qualities. If we wish to refer to moral[53] qualities, we have to use the circumlocution 'human being'. But the adjective 'human', and especially 'inhuman', does refer to moral qualities which human beings are expected to have. Compare also the interestingly different, but closely related, words 'humane' and 'inhumane'.

So the word for 'man' (or 'human being') does have certain values built into it; and when we add the general philosophical reflections about the nature and potentialities of man, we can conclude that we are *not* free to decide for ourselves what man is for, not even what any man, including this man, is for, except within the bounds of these over-riding constraints.

John Stuart Mill said 'No intelligent human being would consent to be a fool, no instructed person would be an ignoramus.'[54] This is a reminder that education has always been a prime concern of all people, at all times and places; and this again points to the objectivity of values. Education just is the organised development of what I have been calling human potentialities, whether physical, moral or intellectual. Of course, not all possibilities can be developed to the limit of each; as Mary Midgley has put it, 'To know what is the good of man we must know [not only] what are his possibilities [but also] roughly what is the price to be paid for each option.'[55] (This is the same point as the fact that the virtues are not fully compatible.) So particular education policies will differ in the weight they attach to different potentialities. Contingency enters at this point; but it must be insisted that it is *not* a contingent fact, which could be otherwise, that it is a matter of supreme importance to us that our children should be educated, and educated in certain ways. Given our knowledge and understanding of what human beings are, we are not free to discard, or to vary without limit, the fundamental concern with what we ought to be.

We have, then, a satisfactory resolution of the problem of form versus content. Both elements are necessary. Morality must, after all, have a certain content; but this content must enter into a certain form (such as universalisable prescriptions). The form is necessary, but not anything of the form will be intelligible as a moral prescription. Both elements are linked by the understanding of what it is to be a human being with a certain possible way of life. And we have a satisfactory continuity with, and a supplementation of, the natural law theory; we are now, as we were not then, in a position both to explain and to justify.

CHAPTER XII

Morality and self-interest

There has been from the beginning of moral philosophy a persistent sceptical thesis which worried Plato, Hobbes, Butler, Kant
and many others; in fact one could almost say that no one can
really be a moral philosopher if he has not at some time been
tempted by the thesis. The thesis is this. From my own point of
view, there are excellent reasons for wanting other people to be
moral, but there are not such obvious reasons for wanting to be
moral myself. Of course I may very well as a matter of fact want to
be moral; most people do; but that is not a *reason why I should* be
moral. I might be better off if I could avoid wanting to be. To put
the point in prescriptivist language: I can easily and sincerely
issue an *all but* universal imperative (everyone, except me, is to do
so and so), but *must* I really include myself among its addressees?
As for my argument in the last chapter, about human potentialities, the sceptic may not be impressed by this appeal: he may be
only too easily absorbed with his own potentiality for amassing
wealth and power, like Plato's tyrant, or the Master Criminal;[56]
and is there any way of convincing him that he must in fact value
what he claims not to value?

The analogy with factual beliefs, which I have relied on at
several points before, will not help here. Certainly a rational
person has no choice but to accept the ordinary standards of
evidence and truth which require him to believe and disbelieve.

He may disagree here and there, he may be an eccentric believer, even a fanatic; but he must believe something; he must commit himself to making judgments about how things are. The only alternative would be to wallow in a sea of sensory impressions, which is simply not a viable alternative to the life of belief. But the sceptics in moral philosophy have recognised several alternatives to the moral life, not all of which are obviously non-viable. Since Kant it is customary to distinguish two important varieties of the non-moral life: inclination, and self-interest. Now of these two, only the first corresponds to the life of sense-impressions without belief, and is as obviously non-viable. Always doing whatever you feel impelled to do on the spur of the moment, without taking a thought even for your own needs and interests, let alone anyone else's, is merely self-destructive. But what about the life of calculated self-interest or rational egoism? This has a large promise of success. And this alternative, rational egoism, is the most plausible alternative to morality.

Plato was so impressed by this version of the sceptical argument that he could think of no way of defending morality against it except by identifying morality with self-interest: a long-term, enlightened self-interest, of course. In behaving morally a man is in fact securing for himself the greatest possible happiness, and the wicked tyrant is not. We may call this the 'Internal Identity thesis': an internal identity between what morality is and what (true) self-interest is. This is opposed to an 'External Identity thesis', which Plato also endorses but regards as unimportant and barely relevant: the thesis that behaving morally has certain consequences, such as praise and the avoidance of sanctions, which a person will incidentally welcome, but which are merely a bonus. The proverb 'Honesty is the best policy' is usually taken to refer to this external identity thesis. Bishop Butler, like Plato, also takes an internal identity view, arguing that the requirements of duty turn out to be identical with the requirements of 'self-love', but adding a heavier chunk of theological comfort for those who do not seem to get their deserts for good conduct in this life – the external thesis again.[57] For Kant, on the other hand, there is the sharpest possible contrast between morality and self-interest; so much so that the pursuit of self-interest is actually described as a case of being unfree (heteronomy, the opposite of autonomy) because it is a matter of being subject to alien pressure, in this case the pressure of wants and needs which are mine, but are external to my true self. Kant points out, quite plausibly, that one can logically wish to have other needs and other desires than the ones one has (someone who is overweight can easily wish he didn't have desires for certain foods), but that it is logically impossible to wish to have different principles. Kant also speaks, in the same vein, of the 'hardened scoundrel'[58] or persistent criminal, who nevertheless, when confronted with shining examples of trust and generosity, wishes that he could have been a man like that. Even Kant mentions rewards in an after-life, thus edging into the external identity thesis, but he makes it very clear that this is not part of ethics, but of cosmology. One must do one's duty whatever the sacrifice to one's own interest may be, even if there is no after-life; it is just that, cosmically speaking, Kant cannot accept a world in which sacrifice is not eventually compensated.[59]

Other writers, including some modern ones, have supported Kant in the view that morality and self-interest are absolutely distinct, and that no appeal can be made to self-interest to back up the claims of morality, since morality is against self-interest. As Mackie puts it, following Warnock:[60]

> Among the factors which contribute to make things go badly in the natural course of things are various limitations – limited resources, limited information, limited intelligence, limited rationality, but above all limited sympathies . . . Men are always more concerned with their selfish ends than with helping one another. The function of morality is primarily to counteract this limitation of men's sympathies.

Let us try to assess these claims about the independence of morality and self-interest. First, we need a clear distinction between the two questions: (1) Why should people be moral? and (2) Why should I be moral? The answer to question 1 is given by Mackie above, and by many others. It is thoroughly in the spirit of Hobbes, dwelling on the evils to be avoided in the state of nature; and it reminds us of the plausibility, so far as it goes, of natural law theory. Obviously it is better for people that people should be moral; and it is better for me that other people should be moral.

[159]

But is it better for me that *I* should be moral? Isn't the best possible world for me, one in which everybody else is dutifully altruistic, and I am the one rational egoist? (It won't be so good, of course, if there are other rational egoists around.) This is question 2, the most searching question raised by the sceptics.

Now from the moral point of view, there is a conclusive reason why I should be moral; indeed this is a tautology. But from the point of view of self-interest, there is a conclusive reason why I should be self-regarding, and this too is a tautology. But from either point of view, the other point of view, it seems, can be ignored or over-ridden. Is there then nothing left but a straight choice between two different and antagonistic points of view? With a real possibility, as we have seen, that egoism might win?

No. Morality *could* win. If morality is to win out over self-interest, we shall have to show that, although morality is in conflict with self-interest, in that it does involve certain sacrifices, it is not in conflict with *ultimate* self-interest. So there is not a *real* sacrifice. To show this we have to show that there is such a thing as a self-interested reason for being moral, though this does not in any way make morality *dependent on*, subsidiary to, self-interest. On the contrary, it shows that only a full understanding of what morality involves can show a person where his true self-interest lies. It shows that the internal identity thesis is true. Well, how can it be shown that a person can, and must, want, need, to be moral – that being moral brings him more happiness or satisfaction, or less unhappiness, in terms that are not question-begging?

Let us first look at two answers which turn out to be inadequate. One appeals to rewards and punishments, secular or religious; the other appeals to the phenomena of personal guilt, shame, or remorse: the inward, as opposed to outward, sanctions. The first answer has already been dealt with under the heading of the external identity thesis. Its inadequacy is well brought out in Plato's imaginative story of Gyges and his magic ring.[61] This is a science-fiction story, but the fiction is a luxury and can be dispensed with. It was only needed in the Gyges case because Gyges was a really extravagant operator in crime. Ordinary common-or-garden moral offences can be kept dark, but killing the king, raping the queen, and taking over the government can hardly be done in secret. But quite a lot of quite serious immorality can be cleverly concealed, and so the sanctions can be avoided, and will not constitute reasons for being moral for anyone, such as the Master Criminal, who can afford to ignore them.

The second answer, in terms of the inner pressures of regret and remorse, might seem to provide better reasons for being moral, because they are inward and so tend to suggest an internal identity between morality and self-interest – in this case, one's interest in avoiding the unpleasantness of a guilty conscience. However, there are at least two objections to relying on these as reasons. One is that we could do a science-fiction job on them, too: instead of a magic ring giving invisibility, all we need is a new type of drug, which might be called a moral tranquilliser, or conscience-killer. Then the pangs of conscience would be no reason for being moral, for anyone who could afford the drugs. The second reason why feelings of guilt and remorse are inadequate is that these are not just 'raw' feelings, which just *happen* to be associated with wrong-doing; they are feelings essentially tied to thoughts; one feels guilty *about* something, and not merely in consequence of it; one feels remorse *for* something; and these feelings would not be the feelings they are, apart from this awareness, the thought, of having done something wrong. If there are no reasons whatever for something being wrong, then it can't *be* wrong, and feeling guilty about it can't be the one and only reason for it being wrong.

So let us pass, finally, to the only kind of argument I can think of which produces a plausible self-interested reason for being moral. This is an appeal to a certain rather special set of needs. We have already seen an explanatory role for certain needs like the need for security. This is an absolutely fundamental and primary one, in the sense that, without the satisfaction of the need for security, no other needs are likely to be satisfied, or even to arise. Yet security depends on *other people's* behaviour being restrained. Our egoist can just exploit this, while leaving his own behaviour unrestrained. What *other* powerful needs might there be, which egoism cannot satisfy?

Consider such things as respect, including self-respect; reciprocated affection; companionship; trust. A life without these will be unimaginably bleak. Yet how can the consistently selfish man get his share, or even any, of these? Even if he gets a response from others which seems like respect, because he has fooled them into thinking that he is an upright and generous person, though all the time he is merely scheming for his own aggrandisement; even if he gets an outward show of respect, how can he possibly value something which he knows is entirely worthless, evoked as it is by a mere pretence? How can he value respect, or the trust of a companion, which is based on deceit? Whatever else he has, he can never achieve *self*-respect and a sense of integrity.

To this simple thesis there are two main objections. First, it might be claimed that there could be someone who does not want any of those things; there could be someone whose life without them might not be bleak. A possible reply to this might be, firstly, that, even if such a case can be imagined, the possibility is of no interest to us, who do value those things. It would have the artificiality of those 'desert-island' problems, where the supposed circumstances are so far removed from the conditions of life as we know it that there is no longer a real question. But there is a stronger reply: we can say that the man who does not want those things *ought* to want them. To be entitled to say that, we would have to resort to what I said in the last chapter about those specifically human attributes and potentialities. We have no choice but to regard someone who really does not care for any of those things as falling short of being fully human.

A second objection is more serious. I said that the consistently selfish man cannot get those valuable things; but, it may be objected, why assume that the selfish man must be *consistently* selfish? Very likely a consistent policy of ruthless self-serving will be self-defeating, but, so the objector claims, this does not prove that isolated acts of wrongdoing, which could be quite serious and frequent, cannot be justified by self-interest, without jeopardising those values. A verbal reply to this objection might be that the original question was 'Why should I be moral?' and *being* moral (or, by contrast, selfish) does imply the consistency of a settled policy or attitude. But this would be a weak reply. We still need to face the harder question, 'Why should I here and now do the thing which is morally right, when it will pay me better to do the wrong thing?' This is the hardest question for a moralist (or moral philosopher) to try to answer (which is why I have left it to the end). First, here is a modern writer who thinks there is indeed no answer:

There is a young bank clerk who decides, quite correctly, that he can embezzle 100,000 dollars without his identity ever being known. He fears that he will be underpaid all his life if he doesn't embezzle, that life is slipping by without his ever enjoying the good things of this world; his fiancée will not marry him unless he can support her in the style of life to which she is accustomed; he wants to settle down with her in a country house, surround himself with books, stereo hi-fi set, and various works of art, and spend a pleasant life, combining culture with sociability. He never wants to commit a similar act again. He does just what he wanted to do; he buys a house, invests the remainder of the money wisely so as to enjoy a continued income from it, marries the girl, and lives happily ever after. He doesn't worry about detection because he has arranged things so that no blame could fall on him; anyway he doesn't have a worrisome disposition and is not one to dwell on past misdeeds; he is blessed with a happy temperament, once his daily comforts are taken care of. The degree of happiness he now possesses would not have been possible had he not committed the immoral act. Apparently, crime sometimes does pay, in fact sometimes it pays very handsomely indeed.[62]

Is there no answer to this up-dated version of the Gyges story? One possible reply might be along these lines. One can deceive everyone else, but one cannot deceive oneself.[63] A bad act committed by any person lowers his moral reputation in the eyes of everyone who knows about it. If no one else does know about it, then his moral reputation is not in fact lowered, except in the eyes of the one person who does know about it, namely himself. This will have two effects, both contrary to his self-interest. First, the respect he enjoys is now more than he deserves, and he knows this; it is based on deceit, even if it is only about a single action; so he has lost something of value to him in self-respect. Second, and perhaps more important, no act can be isolated from the actor. By doing one bad act, he has shown that he is capable of doing bad acts, and he knows this. Worse, it is a matter of common psychology that doing one bad act makes it easier to do others; so this one bad act is likely to be a step in the direction of corruption: in changing his character for the worse; and he knows this. In other words, the objector was not entitled to assume that we can distinguish between a life of consistent immorality, which was admitted to be bad even from the point of view of self-interest, and isolated acts of immorality, which were claimed not to be. So I conclude that we have some sort of answer to the final challenge. It does pay to be moral, and a true concept of morality is the key to where one's true self-interest lies.

Notes

page

  1   1   I shall henceforth make comparatively few concessions to those who dislike the standard English usage whereby 'man' includes both sexes.

  9   2   K. Baier, *The Moral Point of View*, Introduction.

10   3   Attributed to William James.

11   4   Gavin Lyall, *The Most Dangerous Game*.

16   5   *Violence for Equality*, ch.2 ('Our Omissions and their Violence').

27   6   J.S.Mill, *System of Logic*, VI. ii. 2.

32   7   *Freedom and Reason*, p. 185.

40   8   For further discussion of the relation between the right and the good, see p.80, 125.

42   9   *Principia Ethica*, §10.

43 10   Quoted in *Encyclopaedia of Philosophy* (ed. P. Edwards), I, p. 54.

45 11   *Moral Obligation*, p. 9.

46 12   *Zettel*, 717.

49 13   *Language Truth and Logic*, ch. 6.

50 14   p. 38.

50 15   *Principles of Literary Criticism*, ch. 34 ('The Two Uses of Language').

74 16   I use these terms more or less interchangeably, according to context, in order to preserve what continuity there is between older and more recent discussions of relativism.

75 17   Though only to a limited extent, if natural law theory is true: see ch. VII.

87 18   Horace, *Odes* III. 6: Aetas parentum peior avis tulit
                                   nos nequiores, mox daturos
                                   progeniem vitiosiorem.

87 19 Horace again: 'laudator temporis acti'.
92 20 *Moral Luck*, p. 10.
97 21 *Utilitarianism*, ch. 2.
98 22 Plato, *Protagoras*, 322. Writer's translation.
99 23 H.L.A. Hart, *Concept of Law*, ch. 9. My italics.
102 24 *Oedipus Rex*, 1375–1485.
102 25 It is said that certain missionaries engaged in teaching the Lord's Prayer in a matrilinear society used the version 'Our Uncle, which art . . . '.
108 26 *Treatise of Human Nature*, III. i. 1.
109 27 Needless to say, I cannot vouch for the accuracy of this report.
111 28 Kant, *Religion within the Bounds of Pure Reason*, IV, 2, §f15.
111 29 *Utilitarianism*, ch. 2.
112 30 Kant, *Critique of Practical Reason*, Conclusion. Also W.G. Maclagan, *The Theological Frontier of Ethics*.
113 31 *Freedom and Reason*, p. 2.
121 32 I overlook here the technical point that any action required is, strictly speaking, an action under some description, and therefore general; what counts as the same action can differ in points of detail.
121 33 The corresponding reminder of objectivity is harder to elicit, but consider the following: in subjecting others (or myself) to moral appraisal, I make them (or myself) the object of it.
124 34 *Theory of Justice*, p. 20.
124 35 J.L. Mackie, *Ethics*, p. 90.
128 36 G.J. Warnock, *Contemporary Moral Philosophy*, p. 47.
131 37 As noted by G. Ryle (but without attribution to Saki) in 'Forgetting the Difference between Right and Wrong', Melden, *Essays in Moral Philosophy* p. 147.
131 38 Or even to what may, on rare occasions, he called forgetting. I once, after tying my necktie every morning for many years, forgot how to tie it, and remembered three mornings later. (As I was wearing uniform at the time, this was decidedly embarrassing.) We also speak, of course, of forgetting a language.
133 39 Plato, *Euthyphro*, 4 e 4 (Penguin translation).
134 40 A song by Frank Sinatra (which I have been unable to identify) makes this point repeatedly, with lines like 'When I'm not near the girl I love, I love the girl I'm near'.
134 41 'Universalisability', in *Essays on the Moral Concepts*, p. 21.
141 42 By self-interest here I mean what is ordinarily contrasted with morality. The possibility that morality might coincide with 'real' self-interest is discussed in the last chapter.
141 43 The rest of this paragraph is indebted to an article by Prof. C.H. Whiteley, 'On Defining "Moral" ', *Analysis* 20.
144 44 Newspaper report from Cologne, about 1963.

147 45 Plato, *Republic*, 331 b.

148 46 G.J. Warnock, *Contemporary Moral Philosophy*, p. 57.

151 47 Compare the fact that French has no word for kettle.

151 48 There is an excellent example of this functional criterion in a classic science-fiction story, *The Country of the Blind*, by H.G. Wells. The hero, after a climbing accident in the Andes, stumbles into an inaccessible valley, where all the human inhabitants are perfectly adapted to total blindness. Thinking of the proverb 'In the country of the blind, the one-eyed man is king', he expects to be greeted as a superior being, perhaps made a god. Instead he is merely pitied for his incompetence (when he enters a house, which of course has no windows, he falls over people). The doctors diagnose the seat of his disturbed behaviour in two non-functional jelly-like protuberances below his forehead, and recommend surgery . . .

152 49 And likewise of the late President Eisenhower, who had commanded the Anglo-American invasion of German-occupied France, that he was a good general but a bad president.

152 50 Not a formal contradiction, of course, unless we replace 'green' by 'not red'.

154 51 *Republic*, 353 d (strictly, in terms of the 'function' of the *soul*). Also Aristotle, *Nicomachean Ethics*, I. 7.

154 52 Even if only in degree. I do not wish to deny that the rudiments of language and reasoning are to be found in (some) non-human animals.

155 53 This is not meant to deny that specifically male, or female, qualities, if any, may be of moral significance.

155 54 *Utilitarianism*, ch. 2.

155 55 Mary Midgley, Beast and Man, ch. 9.

157 56 G.R. Grice, *The Grounds of Moral Judgment*, p. 101.

158 57 *Sermons*, III §8.

159 58 *Groundwork*, 112.

159 59 *Critique of Practial Reason*, II ii 5.

159 60 *Ethics*, p. 108; Warnock, *The Object of Morality*, p. 26; also K. Baier, *The Moral Point of View*, p. 309. Compare Hart as quoted at p. 97.

160 61 *Republic*, 359.

163 62 John Hospers, *Human Conduct*, pp. 181–2, slightly adapted.

163 63 It may be objected that there is such a thing as self-deception. The topic is highly controversial. Hospers's bank clerk has not, of course, managed to believe that he did not commit the crime at all. The possibility could be discussed. But I doubt whether being self-deceived could ever be in anyone's real interest.

[167]

Further Reading

Classical

Aristotle, *Nicomachean Ethics*
Plato, *Euthyphro; Meno; Republic I*
Butler, J., *Sermons on Human Nature* I–III
Hume, *Treatise on Human Nature* III
Kant, *Groundwork of Metaphysic of Morals* (H.J. Paton, *The Moral Law*)
Mill, J.S., *Utilitarianism*
Moore, G.E., *Principia Ethica*

Contemporary

Baier, K., *The Moral Point of View*
Bambrough, R., *Moral Scepticism and Moral Knowledge*
Bond, E., *Reason and Value*
Frankena, W., *Ethics*
Hare, R.M., *Language of Morals*
Hare, R.M., *Freedom and Reason*
Hare, R.M., *Moral Thinking*
Harman, G., *The Nature of Morality*
Hart, H.L.A., *The Concept of Law*, Ch IX
Hospers, J., *Human Conduct*
Hudson, W.D., *Modern Moral Philosophy*
Mackie, J., *Ethics*
Midgley, M., *Beast and Man*
Murdoch, I., *The Sovereignty of Good*
Nagel, T., *Mortal Questions*

Urmson, J., 'Saints and Heroes' (in Feinberg)
Williams, B., 'Critique of Utilitarianism' (in Smart and Williams),
  Utilitarianism For and Against
Williams, B., *Morality: an Introduction to Ethics*

Collections

Feinberg, J., *Moral Concepts*
Foot, P., *Theories of Ethics*
Hudson, W.D., *New Studies in Ethics* I (Classical Theories)
Hudson, W.D., *New Studies in Ethics* II (Modern Theories)
Rachels, J., *Moral Problems*

Index